Fermenting Everything

ANDY HAMILTON

How to Make Your Own
Cultured Butter, Fermented Fish,
Perfect Kimchi, and Beyond

This volume is intended as a general information resource. Fermenting at home carries certain risks, including contamination of foods and beverages from inadequate cleaning or sanitization of equipment, allergic reactions to ingredients, and use of poisonous plants and leaves. See the Author's Note for a more detailed list of the risks and how to minimize them. This book is not a substitute for advice from a physician or dietician. Before incorporating fermented foods into your diet, especially if you are pregnant or nursing, consult your healthcare provider.

As of press time, the URLs displayed in this book link or refer to existing websites. The publisher is not responsible for, and should not be deemed to endorse or recommend, any website other than its own or any content not created by it; nor is the author responsible for any third-party material in any form.

Manufacturing by RR Donnelley Asia
Series book design by Nick Caruso Design
Production manager: Devon Zahn

Library of Congress Cataloging-in-Publication Data
Names: Hamilton, Andy, 1974– author.
Title: Fermenting everything : how to make your own cultured butter,
    fermented fish, perfect kimchi, and beyond / Andy Hamilton.
Description: First edition. | New York, NY : The Countryman Press, a
    division of W. W. Norton & Company Independent Publishers
    since 1923, [2020] | Series: Countryman know-how | Includes index.
Identifiers: LCCN 2019058901 | ISBN 9781682684696 (paperback) |
    ISBN 9781682684702 (epub)
Subjects: LCSH: Fermented foods. | Fermentation. | LCGFT: Cookbooks.
Classification: LCC TP371.44 .H3525 2020 | DDC 664/.024—dc23
LC record available at https://lccn.loc.gov/2019058901

The Countryman Press
www.countrymanpress.com

A division of W. W. Norton & Company, Inc.
500 Fifth Avenue, New York, NY 10110
www.wwnorton.com

10 9 8 7 6 5 4 3 2 1

Fermenting Everything

THE COUNTRYMAN PRESS

A division of W. W. Norton & Company

Independent Publishers Since 1923

DEDICATION

To my Emma, I don't know why it took five books
for you to get a dedication, but here it is.

AUTHOR'S NOTE

On the following pages you will discover the joy I found in fermenting all kinds of food. I'm very happy to share this joy with everyone—along with my knowledge and experience. But, as I explain at various points in the text, you need to be always aware of certain safety risks and requirements.

Consuming fermented foods: Be careful introducing fermented foods and beverages into your diet. If you are pregnant or nursing or on prescription medication, or if you suffer from any kind of abdominal illness, ask your doctor before you do so. And even if you don't fall into any of those categories, if you find yourself reacting negatively to any fermented product, stop consuming it.

Foraging: To obtain some ingredients for some of these recipes, I recommend foraging. But before you do any foraging, make sure you know what you are looking for and make sure you can recognize poisonous plants and leaves, for example, by reading a field guide that covers your locality or by taking a foraging hike with an expert. *Do not use anything you find foraging as an ingredient unless you are absolutely sure is okay to ingest.*

Mold and "mothers"

- Fermentation involves growing and harnessing microbes. If we get it wrong, we may end up growing the wrong microbes: pathogenic ones that can cause illness. The fermentation process can also produce mold. Both mold and pathogens are dangerous to consume. If you do ingest them as part of your fermented creation, you can get really sick. You also may get sick if mold sticks to the dishware and glassware that you are using.
- You should be able to avoid growing mold or pathogens if you:
  - Follow the procedures in each recipe to the letter.
  - Keep your equipment clean (see below "Cleaning and sanitizing").
  - Do not ferment close to active mold spores.
  - Keep the food submerged below the waterline.
  - Use the right levels of salt or yeast indicated by the recipe.
- How can you spot mold if it does grow despite your best efforts? Mold can be white, black, brown, grey, blue, green, yellow, pink, purple, and/or orange. It grows in dark damp areas.
- Note: Not every white growth is mold. If your creation includes vinegar or kombucha, a white layer that resembles some kind of glue may form on it. That is the start of a "mother" forming, which is a semisolid jelly-like substance that is composed of a form of cellulose and acetic acid bacteria and that develops on fermenting alcoholic liquids and turns alcohol into acetic acid. You don't need to throw out your creation if you see a "mother." What you're seeing also could

be harmless yeast, so refer to the photo of kahm yeast on page 270 before you do anything rash.

- But as a general rule, if you see anything in or on any of your creations that you are not sure is safe, *throw the whole thing out.*

Cleaning and sanitizing

- With many forms of fermentation that I describe in this book, thorough cleaning in a hot dishwasher is usually enough to avoid having mold contaminate your glassware and dishware. But when you are fermenting beverages, the only way to minimize the risk of contamination is by properly sanitizing your equipment at the start and at each step along the way. For that purpose, you can use bleach or other sanitizers, but the sanitizing solution I recommend is an acid-based, no-rinse brand called Star San.
- If, however, despite your best sanitizing efforts, you do see mold in or on one of your creations, again, *throw it out immediately.*

Ingredients

- **Allergies**: If you're fermenting something for yourself, obviously you shouldn't include any ingredient to which you know you're allergic. If you're making something for friends or others, be sure not to serve any product that includes something to which someone else might be allergic, including lactose to someone with a dairy allergy or any product with gluten to someone who is allergic to gluten.

- **Freshness**: Examine apples and other fresh ingredients to make sure they are not stale. Make sure bottled juice or any other packaged ingredient is not past its sale date.

Exploding bottles: You may have heard people talk about exploding home-brew bottles, but the risk of this happening is really, really small as long as you follow the sugar measurements given in the recipes. (To generate an explosion would require exceeding the sugar recommendations by roughly three times the directed amounts.) Also, since such explosions are caused by pressure built up over time, even if there is an explosion, it won't happen while you're actually brewing. It will happen while the brew is being stored. So store your brew bottles in a closed space to lessen the possibility of damage or injury from flying glass if an explosion does occur. Storage in a fridge or a cool store room/cellar will also lower your chances of explosions, since cold temperatures slow down the amount of CO_2 produced that causes explosions.

Injuries from carrying heavy containers: When you make a fermented beverage or even just a large batch of something solid, you may be moving pots of boiling brew around. When you are carrying large containers, be careful not to strain your back.

Burns/scalding: Boiling brew can scald you just like any other boiling liquid, so wear oven mitts and aprons that will protect you even if something does spill.

CONTENTS

Introduction

I grew up in a fairly typical 1980s household; we had a freezer, a microwave, and a VCR—all of which were overused. It wasn't a house full of weird and wonderful jars bubbling and gurgling away. It wasn't a house full of strange and exotic smells, and our refrigerator didn't overflow with jars bursting with flavor and goodness. Yet, this is exactly the house that my own children call home. It's perfectly natural for my three-year-old to ask me, "Is this fermented?" and for my son to tell his friends that Daddy has been "fermenting everything."

Both of my parents worked full time and this meant, like many, we relied on heating up frozen food on weekdays. However, on the weekends with my nan (grandma) we found ourselves baking bread, gardening, foraging for blackberries, picking apples, and living a more natural existence. It was in that atmosphere that I took my first step into fermentation. Sometime back in the early 1980s my mom suggested that we should make ginger beer. The closest our contemporaries came to making homemade

drinks was when they made their own powdered milkshakes, so making our own soda put my mom way ahead of the curve.

I can remember my mom explaining to me that we had to make a starter and that it would "come alive." I must have been around seven years old, and this was true fodder for a childhood imagination. To think, there in our tiny humble kitchen, in a little ceramic pot covered with a tea towel, sat a whole world that was about to come "alive"; like Frankenstein's monster—albeit a much smaller version that wasn't green and didn't have any bolts in its neck.

Almost four decades later I can still recall those feelings of wonderment regarding that very real world living in that ceramic pot. I often wonder if it was that moment that got me interested in fermentation and microbiology, building from a fascination first with yeast and then bacteria. When making kombucha, sauerkraut, boza, or even lacto-fermented orange juice, I can almost feel the personality of the creation forming as each cell comes to life.

These notions of little worlds have always fueled the romantic and poetic side of my nature, and I'm not too ashamed to admit that it took a while before the scientific side caught up. The fact remains, the seven-year-old me didn't ask a very important, fundamental question: "Exactly how does the starter come alive?" I didn't think to ask this question until I returned to brewing at the age of 21—but then again it took humankind generations to ask the same question (see A Short History of Yeast on page 17).

However, I digress, as the great thing about fermenting food and drinks is that you don't have to actually understand the process in order to get started. Some of the recipes in this book are so simple that you may have even accidentally made them in the past! But of course it is good to know what's behind the process.

One of the basic principles in all fermentation is quality control. Your goal is to isolate the chance of any bad stuff getting in and to create the perfect environment for the good stuff to thrive. With yeast (a sugar fungus) you often have to kill off the bacteria. I say *often* because some yeasts work in symbiosis with bacteria during fermentation, as in kombucha for example. For bacterial fermentation, the *lactobacillus* bacteria thrives in a salt solution of 2 to 5 percent. This concentration provides enough salt to dehydrate and kill off any harmful bacteria and leave the salt-tolerant good bacteria. Last, there is mold fermentation, such as koji (a mold used to ferment soybeans and grains). In order to get the good guys winning here you need to create the perfect conditions for the mold to thrive. To do so, humidity and temperature need to be perfectly managed.

Koji fermentation is demanding, and I do not include it in this book. I made a decision to only include recipes that can be reproduced in many different climates without needing a master's degree in fermentation. It is possible to make koji at home, but I think it really needs a lot more space than I can give it here.

Indeed, each of these fermentation processes could warrant their own book, but by following the recipes and the advice I give throughout this book, by the end you might feel like you have your own master's degree in fermentation! If you are still hungry (or thirsty) to find out more, then turn to the back pages of this book. There you'll find listings for a host of books, websites, and resources that will help you once you too start *Fermenting Everything*!

CHAPTER 1

What Were the First Fermented Foods?

A few years back, articles appeared in some of the less reputable newspapers and websites around the world offering proof that time travel existed. The headlines were all a variation on "Mummy Found Wearing Adidas." Sure enough, at first glance the mummy did seem to be wearing shoes with the distinct Adidas stripes, and they also seemed to be made to fit around the foot just like real sneakers. What it really proved was just how sophisticated ancient Egyptian cobblers were and how, no matter how new we think things are, some technologies have been with humankind for a lot longer than we think.

I see fermented food in a similar light. Right now, we seem to be going through a huge revival of what, in truth, are ancient techniques and recipes. We may have better ways to communicate and therefore have access to more recipes, but the basic principles of these recipes remain the same. The mummy in those Adidas sneakers might well have enjoyed essentially the same foods that are currently found at some of the most cutting-edge restaurants in the world. He may have woken up every morning and had a yogurt, jogged to his place of work, eaten a lunch of sourdough bread with some simple curd cheese, and then washed it down with a glass of sour beer all before clocking out and heading to an Egyptian nightspot to sink a few glasses of mead with his friends who all sported carefully sculpted beards. In

other words, this ancient hipster could be living the same life as your on-trend, cutting-edge person from Portland, Oregon, or Shoreditch in East London.

As well as being ancient, fermented foods and drinks can be found across the planet. When something is this entwined within human culture, the question that should be asked is, Did it exist prehuman? Primate behavior can help to elucidate, and if the chimps of Bossou, Guinea, are anything to go by, then our primate ancestors may well have been booze hounds! The local drink of Bossou is naturally fermented raffia palm sap. The locals tap the palms close to the crown and let the sap drip into containers where it ferments. The chimps will rob around a quart of this fermented sap at a time, the equivalent to drinking half a bottle of wine or three beers. Far from being just fun, it's thought that this might give them an advantage over chimps that don't drink. This is because alcohol slows down metabolism and promotes fat storage, which we might consider a problem but is an advantage in the wild.

Can we look elsewhere? It might seem odd, but

scientists often study the fruit fly to give an insight into our own genome (we share around 44 percent of the same DNA with fruit flies). According to a 2017 study first published in the respected journal *Science,* it would seem that male fruit flies turn to booze if they can't find a mate, mirroring human behavior in many late night bars across the world!

The enjoyment of fermented products may well be fused deep within the psyche of much of the fauna on this planet, but that doesn't start to answer just how long humans have been fermenting their foods and drinks. The truth is, we may never know the exact whos, whys, and whens behind the origins of fermented foods. We can, however, look upon archeological fragments that contain the mere snippets of information about indigenous peoples' diets, aspects of which have remained unchanged, certainly for centuries if not for millennia. It is through this window, which in reality is tiny and blurred, that we can steal a momentary glance upon a foodscape that is thousands of years old. The diet of the first people to inhabit what is now the United States shows an interesting insight, and in northern regions of the continent we have found some indication that meat may have been fermented underwater during the last Ice Age. The sea is an ideal medium for fermented food, as it has a salinity of 3 to 5 percent, the exact range needed. This one finding may be an indicator of a much more widespread practice.

We don't really have what we could call *hard evidence* of fermented foods until the birth of agriculture. This evidence comes in the form of a kind of gruel, some say beer, found in Israel. It is thought to be around 13,000 years old. The domestication of animals helped to create the next oldest fermented food, which we speculate is cheese. Fragmental evidence was found in Iraq and is thought to be about 9,000 years old.

Fast forward another 5,000 to 6,000 years. Other milk and meat products were starting to be made, the most sophisticated of which was perhaps sausages. These were first made by the ancient Babylonians in 1500 BC. About 1,000 years later the fermentation bug had spread to China, where they started to make something we might recognize as tofu. It wasn't until around 2,300 years ago that the Chinese progressed to fermenting vegetables. Meaning that sauerkraut and kimchi are relative newcomers to the fermented foods family!

I hope the next time you find yourself in a trendy café that's selling their new fermented foods, you think back to that Adidas-wearing Egyptian. You can smile to yourself at just how old new trends can be.

A Short History of Yeast

Our ancestors believed that yeast spontaneously came into being. They knew yeast as goddisgoode (god is good), from the simple blessing they gave their brews, "bicause it cometh of the grete grace of God" (because it comes of the great grace of God). They had no idea that yeast could be cultivated or that they could use different strains to do different jobs. There were no bread yeasts, wine yeasts, or beer yeasts. This was also reflected in law. A great example is the German beer purity law act (*Reinheitsgebot*) of 1516. It listed only three ingredients for making beer: water, malt, and hops. No yeast!

It wasn't until the 17th century, when a Dutch tradesman named Antonie van Leeuwenhoek developed the first crude microscopes, that humans first started to see yeast. He loved looking at these other worlds and would invite the great and good around to his house to have a look too. No one knew where these cells came from and many thought they just "came alive."

Then in the 19th century came along the great French chemist Louis Pasteur, who was credited with being the first person to realize that yeast did not spontaneously form but that it was present in nature. In his 1857 paper *Mémoire sur la fermentation alcoolique,* he wrote about his series of experiments with alcoholic fermentation. These experiments either killed the yeast cells off by boiling or kept them alive in a swan-necked container to minimize contamination. His boiling experiments of course sterilized the environment and killed off the yeast cells; but in the ones that were not boiled, the yeast fermented. He went on to conclude that boiling killed the yeast and that it needed to be alive for alcoholic fermentation to occur, something that seems obvious to us today.

It seems totally bizarre now, in our rational, scientific world, that the commonly held belief for most of humankind's existence was that life could spontaneously appear. It was a suitable explanation to why spoiling meat gave birth to maggots, why milk could turn to yogurt, and how beer could be produced from water, malt, and hops.

A Very Short History of Fermented Beverages

Was the first-ever fermented beverage an accident? Did ancient humans drink moldy grape liquid one day and discover that it gave them a buzz? It is impossible to know, but evidence suggests that we have been drinking for many generations. The earliest evidence of wine dates back to Asia, in Georgia, around 8,000 years ago; fermented honey drink mead can be dated to 9,000 years ago in ancient China; and evidence of beer dates back to around 13,000 years ago in a cave in Israel. Other drinks are much younger: Evidence of kefir dates to around 1,900 years ago in the Caucasus mountains, and kombucha is thought to have originated around the same time too.

The yeast and bacteria strains that evolved to feed off the sugars to make these drinks have been around long before mankind started to walk upright. Indeed, yeast has been around for hundreds of millions of years, and bacteria has been knocking about for billions of years. It's quite possible that our love affair with fermented drinks started with proto-humans. Because naturally occurring alcohol from fermenting fruit predates humans, perhaps the first humanlike person to enjoy a fermented beverage happened upon it by accident. We can only imagine what this discovery must have felt like, and it makes us wonder if that person wanted more.

There is a theory that civilization itself started because of our love of beer. Some suggest that we may have started farming because we wanted to grow wheat and barley to make beer. The storing of these cereal crops led to settlements and a hierarchical culture, things that we associate with our civilized society. It is also true that the earliest evidence of what could be called a cookbook is linked to our joy of fermented beverages. This "book" is actually a clay tablet with marks in it. Each mark represents a word—rather like the Chinese written language. As archeologists continued to find these clay tablets, they determined that each seemed to be a written recording of goods, perhaps for a tax audit. But one tablet was different. This 4,000-year-old lump of clay contains a recipe that turned bread into beer. (For my recipe based on this, see A Simple All-Grain Beer on page 192.) The recipe belonged to the ancient and great civilization of Mesopotamia. Interestingly, we have no evidence of a civilization that preceded this one. Therefore, fueled by a love of beer, these people were instrumental for creating what we call the civilized world.

Our love of beer still continues, of course. It is one of the most widely consumed drinks in the world. But there is more to fermented drinks than the mix of barley, water, yeast, and hops. Indeed,

most cultures seem to have their own fermented beverage. These range from boza (fermented bulgur wheat) in Turkey, *sollip-cha* (fermented pine needles) in Korea, and kvass (fermented rye bread) in Russia.

Health Benefits of Fermentation

There is a vast ecosystem living in our gut. This ecosystem comprises bacteria, yeast, fungi, viruses, and protozoans. This world is known as the gut microbiome, and it can weigh up to 4 pounds (2 kg). This is heavier than the combined weight of your lungs, heart, pancreas, and kidneys.

These life forms have coevolved within us over millions of years, and scientists are only now starting to discover that they are vital for our digestion and immune system. This means if you don't have a healthy gut microbiome, your health may suffer. It also means that, at some point in the not-so-distant future, health insurance companies might be more interested in your poo than in your genes.

Research into this area is a hot topic, and five times more papers about it have been published in medical journals this decade than in the last 40 years. Although the importance of a healthy gut microbiome has been clearly established, how to actually keep it healthy is the cause of great debate. There are plenty of people out there who claim that fermented foods are a panacea, a cure-all, and that they will save us from everything from irritable bowel syndrome (IBS) to Crohn's disease. Is there any truth to these claims? Can sauerkraut really relieve abdominal pain? Can kefir make you happy? Will kimchi make you skinny? Can all these health benefits be attributed to fermented food and drink?

The short answer is maybe. Considering that each individual is unique, that the microbiome is more complex than we fully understand, and how little we understand about the bacteria in our food and in ourselves, any emerging evidence needs to be considered carefully and not just taken at face value.

In the West, our approach to medicine and our health is rather reductionist. That is, we tend to look for yes-and-no answers to our problems. But quite often we come across "maybe" and "not sure" answers. I firmly believe that, if we keep looking, we will find that an ingestion of our local bacteria will help our bodies toward better health. Locally sourced organic and wild food are teeming with good-for-you bacteria, and eating them returns you to an approximation of a *traditional* diet.

On a personal note, I suffer from an autoimmune disease affecting my kidneys. I have been an outpatient taking medication for many years. When the condition flares up at its worst I can only be active, and mildly active at that, for 45 minutes a day. What's more, I can put on up to 28 pounds in excess fluid and can experience a period of low energy that can lead to weight gain.

Because I am only able to have very short meetings with my specialist, I decided to do my own research. I painstakingly decoded some of the medical papers out there on this condition and other autoimmune diseases. Although the findings are not conclusive (science rarely is), I found there to be a correlation between infants who were fed unsweetened condensed milk or evaporated milk and an increase in autoimmune diseases. In the 1970s, when I was born, mothers who did not breast feed their babies were advised to feed them condensed milk. I was one of those non-breast-fed babies.

The reason for the correlation is that those infants struggle to create a biologically diverse gut biome. I also found that some doctors were suggesting that my particular autoimmune condition was possibly caused by rogue bacteria. Reading, then, that the Hadzabe tribe of Tanzania—one of the last remaining hunter-gatherer tribes—had such a robust and diverse gut biome that they could keep three strains of E. coli in perfect balance, I realized that although I cannot cure my condition through my diet, my future health could at least be improved by trying to improve my gut bacteria. Since that realization I have included fermented food in my diet and upped my soluble fiber intake on a daily basis. As a result I feel generally healthier and am more able to tackle the condition when it does flare up and the side effects of the medication.

The main thing when it comes to your health is to listen to your own body. If you feel yourself reacting negatively to a fermented food or drink, despite all of the health claims you may have read, then simply stop consuming it. If you feel that a food or drink is doing you some good, then by all means carry on. If you are drinking kombucha by the gallon every day and are feeling bloated or even a bit drunk, then use a bit of common sense and cut back. Anything in excess isn't good for the complex machine that is a human being. For example, I find that an excess of kefir just doesn't feel right to me. I can't put my finger on what changes, but I just instinctively know something isn't right.

So what are the facts about fermented food and drink? What can be gleaned from the massive increase of interest in them?

As it turns out, what's new is very old. For centuries and perhaps eons, plenty of anecdotal evidence has accumulated to suggest that fermented foods can improve health. Look into the diet of most traditional cultures and you'll see that fermented food and drink are part of the diet. You'll also see lower rates of depression and reduced levels of many other Western diseases. I personally notice a mood change when I eat fermented foods; or, to be exact, I notice an increase in anxiety and depression when I don't ingest fermented foods. I also notice more digestion problems and decreased energy levels when I don't ingest fermented foods. I am not alone. The Internet is currently buzzing with bloggers, YouTubers, and the like who all attribute their good health to fermented food. But could all this be attributed to the placebo effect?

I considered the mood-enhancing effects that I feel when I have ingested fermented food. I wondered if these mood changes had been in my head. It wasn't.

It turns out that they are most likely in my gut. This is because 95 percent of the neurochemical serotonin, one of our happiness neurochemicals, is created in the digestive tract (or gut). Can the gut be manipulated into creating more serotonin by eating or drinking fermented foods? In a study published in 2011, a strain of the bacteria *Lactobacillus rhamnosus* was administered to seemingly healthy mice under stress. It was found there was a reduction in anxiety and depression-like behaviors in the rodents. However, because mice are not humans a follow-up study was conducted. *Lactobacillus casei* was given to 132 healthy people for three weeks, and it was found that they all reported an elevated mood. It would appear that fermented foods can make you happier. [1]

I decided to look further into the data available. I came across a claim that stated fermented foods can lessen or reduce symptoms for allergy sufferers. There are a variety of conditions that fall into this category (including food allergies, asthma, and eczema), and cases of these are going up across the planet. Any relief would, of course, be welcomed by sufferers. After some searching, I found a paper by Elizabeth Furrie from the Department of Immunology at the University of Dundee in Scotland. She found that the Western lifestyle can cause an imbalance in a newborn's immune system. Using the data from two in-depth studies, she concluded that through the use of probiotic ther-

---

1   Bravo JA, Forsythe P, Chew MV, Escaravage E, Savignac HM, Dinan TG, Bienenstock J, Cryan JF. "Ingestion of Lactobacillus strain regulates emotional behavior and central GABA receptor expression in a mouse via the vagus nerve." *PNAS* 2011 Sep 20; 108(38): 16050–5.

apy, which includes the introduction of lactobacilli, milk allergies and eczema can be controlled. This is because probiotic therapy can help with the colonization of a healthy gut. [1]

Does this mean a nursing mother should try to include fermented foods into her diet? I'd suggest that it does, but only under the strict supervision of a health-care professional, as pregnant and nursing mothers are more at risk to infection. Should adults with allergies increase their consumption of fermented food and drink? Unfortunately, the evidence for the probiotics in fermented foods helping adult allergy sufferers is as yet inconclusive.

I think fermented foods for allergy sufferers fits into the *sort-of-true* camp, but I am sure that you don't want to base your health-care decisions on findings that are *sort of true*. You want cast-iron truths about how fermented foods will improve your life. But if you suffer from IBS, there is some very good news for you. In three clinical trials lasting four weeks, patients taking probiotics found relief from their abdominal pain after taking probiotics, as compared to those taking a placebo. What's more, flatulence and bloating showed a decrease after taking probiotics. Interestingly, studies have shown that the bloating can increase again with long-term use. The takeaway then? Eat fermented food when your IBS flares up, then ease off for a bit when your quality of life improves.[2]

One of the most intriguing claims about fermented food is that it helps you lose weight. Another study using mice found that slimmer and nondiabetic mice had more of the bacteria *A. muciniphila* than obese and diabetic mice. In order to kick-start *A. muciniphila,* you need to feed it fructans, a chain of molecules found in many foods such as wheat, garlic, and onions. Fermentation can increase the bioavailability of fructans, as the fermentation process breaks down the plant fibers of foods high in fructans so that the body can absorb more. In other words, foods such as fermented garlic might just be helping to keep you trim.

There are almost as many reported health benefits to eating fermented foods as there are recipes in this book. However, I hope that by describing just a few health benefits, I have outlined for you just how complex a subject it is. I hope too that the recipes in this book point you in a direction that leads to better health and happiness for yourself and your loved ones. However, I am not a doctor or a dietitian. I am an individual who eats and drinks fermented food on a regular basis and who believes it is doing me some good. Before you start to eat fermented food in the hope that it will cure anything, just remember that we are all unique and wonderful in our own right and what might be right for some people might not be right for others. If you are on medication or have an underlying

1   Furrie E. "Probiotics and allergy." *Proc Nutr Soc.* 2005 Nov; 64(4): 465–9.
2   Didari T, Mozaffari S, Nikfar S, Abdollahi M. "Effectiveness of probiotics in irritable bowel syndrome: Updated systematic review with meta-analysis." *World J Gastroenterol.* 2015 Mar 14; 21(10): 3072–3084.

medical condition and are not sure about adding fermented foods to your diet, then please talk to a medical practitioner before you start fermenting anything.

Fermentation Gear

Most houses have a drawer, cupboard, or even cellar that contains gadgets we're convinced we can't live without. Electric carving knives, twirling spaghetti forks, taco holders, or pizza scissors spring to mind. In actual fact, we don't need these items cluttering up our lives.

Unfortunately, many future landfill items are out there for the would-be fermenter too. Don't be fooled—you don't need to spend any money at all to get into food fermenting. Once you get into the swing of fermenting, you won't need anything more than a jar and items that you probably already have hanging around in your kitchen. I've successfully fermented everything from sauerkraut to a joint of beef without the need for anything other than a jar I pulled out of a recycling bin.

That said, there are a few things that will come in handy. If money is tight (or you are), but you have a well-stocked kitchen, then you will already have most of the items you need. If you do need to buy a few things, then rest assured that, if you buy right, they will last a lifetime.

Jars and Crocks: There are a few different makes of jars on the market and, to be honest, there is lit- tle difference among them. Your choices will boil down to personal preference. The screw-top canning jar with a two-piece lid is the go-to jar in the United States. The rubber-ringed, flip-top jar tends to be favored in Europe.

They both have their merits. The screw-top mason jars or Ball jars have a host of accessories that fit them perfectly, such as lids with airlocks and glass weights. What's more, because they have been around for 130 years or more, they are easy to procure. You can start by looking through the back of relatives' cupboards or thrift stores. However, if you can get a hold of some flip-top jars, do so. I highly recommend that you get at least one or two. These have a number of benefits: first, you can be certain that no metal will taint your ferment, as these have glass lids. Second, you can take off the rubber seal and loosely fit the lid when conducting the first stage of fermentation, reducing the need for covering with a tea towel. Last, over time, the lids from mason jars tend to rust, meaning you have to buy new ones or run the risk of ruining a fermentation. Even if the metal casing starts to rust on your flip-top jars, you can still use them, as no metal comes into contact with the contents in the jar.

Throughout this book I specify the size of jar that you need for each ferment. This is a guideline only, and the keen eyed will notice that some of the photos don't match up with the recommended jar. This is because I often start making a ferment only to find that all of my jars are half full and sitting in my refrigerator. I then have to resort to using what-

fermented product. A honey jar in particular can retain some of the original flavor of the honey, and I have no doubt they contain some pollen and yeast cells too. A couple of runs through the dishwasher or a thoroughly good scrubbing will sort out this problem.

Another option is to use any crock you can get your hands on. For a cover, simply use a small plate covered with rocks to press down on the contents. It is easier to get crocks that are at least a quart in size if not bigger, and using these larger crocks means you will need to adjust the recipes accordingly. A trip to your local thrift store could prove very fruitful!

Water Lock Crocks (optional): There is an array of beautiful water lock crocks out there. Not only do they look great on your countertop, but many are designed perfectly to ferment. However, the downside of these crocks is the price. Some will set you back at the cost of the weekly minimum wage!

That said, the technology is sound and many of the specially crafted crocks are produced using ancient techniques. Also, plenty of artisanal potters are out there making these crocks, and you could really help an emerging cottage industry by buying at least one of these crocks new. They are not ideal for every ferment, but if you love kimchi or sauerkraut and make it in any quantity, then they are certainly worth the investment.

Water lock crocks look like any ceramic jar with a lid. You make your ferment and put it inside. The crock should come with two weight stones. These stones fit together to form a perfectly round covering

ever jars I have knocking around, often old jam, olive, or honey jars.

Any size jar can, of course, be used to ferment, and recipes need to be adjusted accordingly. I would suggest that you trust your nose when working out if the previous contents of the jar will affect your finished for your fermented vegetables. Water laps over the top of the stones through a doughnut-shaped hole in the middle. A lid fits inside a groove at the top of the crock. Pouring in a little water around this creates a "moat" that the lid rests on, forming an airtight seal. Simple and effective!

Tea Towel or Small Piece of Material: For many of the recipes in this book you'll notice I suggest covering your fermentation jar. This is in order to keep out any bugs. It need not be anything fancy. I use old and frayed shirts that I cut into pieces.

Airlocks: Specialty airlocks are available, and these fit neatly onto mason jars and Ball jars. They are useful because they minimize the amount of air that gets to your fermentation and thus helps to minimize spoilage. However, good practice negates the need for them. That said, they may be a godsend if you live in a small apartment as they can reduce the unpleasant odors that are sometimes released during the art of fermentation!

Knife: A knife is the single most important item in any kitchen, as the preparation of most dishes starts with a knife. Other than a bread knife, you don't really need more than two blades in a domestic kitchen. One blade should be 4 inches (10 cm) long and the other should be at least 9 inches (20 cm) long. The longer blade is useful for cutting into bigger vegetables like cabbages, and also when cutting meat. The shorter blade is useful for cutting finer items like

herbs, garlic, or for filleting fish. It's important too that you choose a knife that is comfortable in your hand. If it doesn't feel right, you won't use it. I suggest going to a kitchen shop for your knives (rather than buying over the Internet) so that you can at least pick up the knives and see how they feel in your hand.

Avoid buying knives with flimsy handles. I've made this mistake and I can honestly say the "buy cheap, buy twice" rule certainly applies to knives!

It's important that you look after your knives. Never wash your knives in the dishwasher, as the temperature changes, detergents, and agitation from the high-powered water jets can all take their toll on knife sharpness. Also, knives need to be stored on a magnetic strip or in a wooden block. Leaving knives loose in a kitchen drawer can dull the blades.

Knife Sharpener: If a knife is the most important tool in the kitchen, then the second most important is a knife sharpener. The importance of keeping a sharp knife shouldn't be underestimated. It can save you hours over the course of a year and, perhaps, even save you from injury, because you compensate for a dull blade by adding more force, and more force can mean an injurious slip.

There are a variety of knife-sharpening tools on the market and each works slightly differently. I use a steel and sharpen my blades every time I use them. Hold your knife at 45 degrees and run the whole of the blade down the steel, ensuring you do this on both sides. If using an expensive Japanese knife, you may consider using a whetstone. Other options include electric sharpeners and pull throughs. Again, visit a kitchen shop and talk to them about what suits you.

Grater or Mandoline: Having a cheese grater means that you can get your vegetables and roots processed to a fairly uniform size and shape. This can be useful when making quicker sauerkrauts, because the smaller surface area obtained by grating speeds up the fermentation process. A mandoline does a similar job but creates longer, uniform ribbons. It can take a while to get used to using it without cutting your fingers.

Both graters and mandolines are worth investing in, and if you do, then go midrange or higher. Cheaper versions of both will fall apart and can even become dangerous if you intend to use them frequently.

Food Processor or Hand Blender: A food processor can be really useful when making big batches of things. However, my personal preference is to use a hand blender, a knife, or a mortar and pestle. I like to feel what I am doing as I process my food. However, when I am short on time or I have a big batch of ogi or crème fraîche to blend into cultured butter, then I prefer using a food processor. I'd suggest making the recipes first as best you can with the tools you have before you go out and buy something. You want to make sure fermenting gets incorporated into your daily life before you start investing in expensive specialty tools.

Pounding Sticks/Rolling Pins: I've never really seen the point in buying a specialty bit of equipment to crush my kraut. Instead, I use a one-piece French-style tapered rolling pin. I simply use either end of it to crush my vegetables. It also works well for making pasta and as a cocktail muddler! They are available online or at specialty baking shops. Don't be fooled into spending too much money on one—they should be available for less than the cost of two draught beers.

Measuring Spoons: Don't be fooled into thinking that a normal household spoon will do the job as, unfortunately, there is no uniform size for them. Therefore, it is highly advisable that you use a set of actual measuring spoons so that you do not add too much or too little salt to your ferment.

You should be able to pick up an inexpensive plastic set from most hardware stores. You can get a slightly more expensive set of stainless steel ones from a good kitchen store or the Internet. The latter should last you a lifetime.

Weights, Mini Plates, or Zip-Top Bags: Most of the recipes in this book involve keeping produce below the waterline to protect it from airborne mold. Various options are available here. My friend Martin, who runs fermentation workshops, uses tiny saucers from espresso coffee cups with some stones on top of them. You can also buy glass "stones" that fit exactly in the mouth of a Ball jar or mason jar. These are my preferred method as they are fairly easy to use—I say fairly because there is a knack to taking them out of the jar. I tend to drain off any liquid first and then maneuver them out. Don't try to pry them out with a knife as it will shatter the glass and ruin whatever is inside the jar, something I found out the hard way.

Other, cheaper options include zip-top bags—these can be placed over the top of your ferment with enough water inside them to keep them in place. I'm not totally comfortable recommending plastic, but the fact remains that this method works very well.

I've also been known to use a plastic bag or food plastic wrap with some stones on the top. Whatever you decide to use, just ensure that it doesn't contain metal, as this can taint the flavor. Also, be sure it's clean and not contaminated, and that it will keep the contents of the jar below the waterline.

Fermentation Vessel: The first brewers would have used anything that could hold liquid to ferment, from animal skins to carved wooden bowls, and even earthen pits. I am not suggesting that you do this, but what I am suggesting is that you can use your imagination before parting with your hard-earned dollars. As long as it is food grade, scratch free, nonmetallic (unless stainless steel), and can be sterilized, then you can use any vessel that will hold liquid without leakage. I have used storage boxes, food-grade food buckets, and even a large stainless steel pot that someone was chucking out.

If you do decide to go for a fermentation vessel, think about what job you need to use it for, as they come in a variety of sizes. The smallest sizes are plenty large for making kefir, kombucha, boza, and small batches of wine. The larger sizes are more useful for making hard cider and beer.

If you plan to brew both kombucha and beer or cider, then it is advisable to keep your fermentation vessels separate. That is, your kombucha vessel should be used for kombucha, your beer vessel for beer, and so forth.

Bottles: Not all bottles are created equal! From experience I would steer clear of reusing screw-top bottles for anything other than the short-term fermentation. This is because the contents in such bottles quickly spoil.

Flip-top bottles are advisable for making kombucha, lacto-fermented drinks, and elderflower champagne. These bottles are specially designed to pop open if too much gas builds up inside. Steer clear of cheap copies with thin metal clasps and even thinner glass, as these are more likely to explode.

Beer bottles with crown caps are my preferred bottle of choice for beer. It keeps the beer in good condition and the bottles can be bought cheaply or even obtained for free by keeping your empties, asking a local bar for theirs, or getting your drinking buddies to hold a few back for you.

For wine I like to use old wine bottles with corks pushed into them. Cork has been used for centuries as it helps the wine to breathe a little, which gives aged wine more character.

Corking Machine and Crown Cappers: If bottling up, then a crown capper is essential. You can get by with using crown caps and a hammer, but your fingers will thank you for getting a crown capper. They can be bought at good homebrew stores and from the Internet. Unless you plan on opening a brewery, I'd suggest you don't need to spend a fortune to get a good-enough crown capper.

I would also suggest that a good lever-operated corking machine is invaluable for wine. Again, steer clear of anything that involves using a hammer near glass!

SPECIALTY EQUIPMENT

For some of the recipes, all-grain beer for example, you will need specialty equipment. Some of the fermenting equipment available on the market is very necessary, but some of it falls into the camp of informercial rubbish. I hope to help you discern which is which. Also, when buying equipment remember to check out websites that sell second-hand goods or give a shout-out on social media. I have known people who have gotten complete brewing kits for free because the person giving them away needed to free up some space. Don't ever be afraid to ask.

Carboys/Demijohns: These are the glass containers used for fermenting liquids; they are sometimes known as jugs. They come in a variety of sizes, from a single gallon (4 L) up to 5 gallons (25 L). The top tapers in and can be plugged with a rubber bung with an airlock. They allow air out but prevent oxygen and bacteria from getting in.

A carboy's prime use is as a secondary fermentation vessel, after the fermentation has slowed down. Finishing a ferment in a carboy often helps with conditioning a drink and avoiding explosions in bottles.

They can be bought either at your local homebrew shop or online. Due to their bulky nature, carboys are often one of the first things a retired homebrewer will rid themselves of, and so second-hand carboys are easily found at yard sales, from online sources, and in thrift stores.

Wort Chiller: There are three different types of wort chillers: immersion chillers, counter-flow chillers, and plate chillers (which are essentially very small, very efficient counter-flow chillers).

Immersion chillers are made of long metal pipes, normally copper, which is coiled. The coil is dunked into the boiling wort (unfermented beer) and cold water passes through the metal tubing; because it has a large surface area, the pipe rapidly cools. Warm water runs out of the other end of the tube as the heat is sucked out of the wort. It is like having cold feet put on your hot leg in the middle of the night!

A counter-flow chiller is also a coil but with some silicone covering it. Cold water is pumped through the silicone and the wort is siphoned through the inner piping in the opposite direction. This cools the wort very quickly.

Plate chillers are awesome. They work using the same counter-flow principle, but instead they do it on a micro-scale. They can chill from 212°F to 64°F (100°C to 18°C) in the blink of an eye.

All of the above can be bought at your preferred homebrewer supplier. However, both immersion and counter-flow chillers can be made at home. I'd suggest looking for online videos for ideas on how to make yours.

Mash Tun: To release the sugars from a grain, the grain mash needs to be kept at a regular, controlled temperature for an allotted period of time. This is normally done with a specialty bit of equipment called a mash tun. The cheapest way of doing this is by using an insulated cooler. Some people affix a little tap on the bottom of the cooler in order to drain out the liquor. There are plenty of videos available online showing how to make one at home. If you are feeling less adventurous, you can buy a mash tun.

Fermentation Techniques

Put what you want to ferment in a vessel, add brine, yeast, and/or starter culture, and then leave it until you like the taste. Really, that's all the advice you need when fermenting. So please, if you have never fermented anything, let alone *everything,* don't be afraid. It's easy!

That said, to ensure that the families of microorganisms that you are cultivating get the best life possible, there are a few dos, a few don'ts, and some simple little techniques to follow.

CHOOSING INGREDIENTS
Remember that food fermentation isn't about using up the wilted leaves at the back of the refrigerator or that battered fruit with an army of flies making camp in it. It's about preserving and locking in nutrients. If you use lackluster cabbage, you'll get lackluster sauerkraut. If you use the freshest possible foods, not only will the final product taste better but you will have locked in more nutrients.

HARD-TO-FIND INGREDIENTS
I believe that wherever possible domestic ingredients should be used instead of imports, as local ingredi-

ents tend to be fresher and so retain more nutrients. In addition, local products require less fuel to get from field to plate, which means less pollution in the air. As a result, we can all breathe a little more easily.

That said, there are many recipes in this book from faraway lands. It might not always be possible to find substitute ingredients, though I provide suggestions when possible in these recipes. If you live in a larger city, then you hopefully should be able to find these ingredients at ethnic or whole food stores. If you live deep in the countryside, then you may have to have some of these ingredients shipped to you. Consult the resources section at the back of the book for suggested online resellers.

If you have the space, then you could always try to grow some of the fruits, vegetables, and herbs you ferment. These will of course be the freshest possible ingredients, because you can ferment them almost as soon as they are harvested.

ORGANIC, SOIL-GROWN VERSUS INDOOR-GROWN VEGETABLES

My Korean chef friend and other fermentation gurus recommend using only soil grown vegetables as opposed to hydroponic and aeroponic vegetables. This is because some of the bacteria needed for fermentation is present in soil. Indeed, one of the challenges of growing vegetables indoors can be a huge increase of pathogens. Just imagine for a second an environment where all of the plants in it share the same water and the same air. If one plant gets sick, the rest will too. It is kind of like being on a bus or a plane with someone sneezing on the entire trip—you know you'll have that cold in the next few days!

In order to fight these pathogens, some indoor growers add humic and lactic acids to their nutrient mix, and it does seem to help. In other words, these growers are trying to mimic some of the conditions that the plant would experience naturally. Does this mean that indoor plants will be home to as many nutrients and microorganisms as organically and sun-grown vegetables? Well, the only real answer I can give right now is that we don't know. There is big money in indoor growing, and I have no doubt that this is how much of the food of the future will be grown. This means money is being poured into making it work. I know that outdoor, soil-grown, organic food tastes better. I also know when I have an abundance of organic food that I feel I have more energy. Granted, these assessments are less than scientific, and until there are more credible studies on the nutritional value of organically and soil-grown food versus indoor-grown food, I'm afraid to say the jury is out. So you'll have to make your own decision and these may be based more on your own personal ethics and values than anything else.

As I have already mentioned, if you have the space, growing your own is an option. Knowing your food from seed to table is pretty life-affirming, and I would highly recommend it (again).

DECHLORINATING WATER

For many of the recipes in this book you'll see that unchlorinated water is suggested. If you don't know

if your water supply is chlorinated or not, then check your water company's website. I'd wager that it is, unless you get your water from some other source such as a well, spring, or bore hole.

The easiest way to remove chlorine is by *off-gassing*, which means letting your water sit for 24 hours so that the chlorine evaporates. If you get into a routine with your ferments, then this will become easy. However, not everyone is that organized and many water authorities are now adding a secondary treatment of chloramine, which remains even after off-gassing. Luckily, there are other options.

A slightly quicker way to dechlorinate is to boil the water for 15 minutes. This is especially useful if making brine, as you will be boiling the water any-way in order to dissolve the salt. Always make sure you let your water cool to about room temperature before using. Again, this doesn't remove chloramine.

Another option is to purchase a water filter that will remove chlorine. These vary in price and useful-ness. Do your homework before purchasing. Some have the added bonus of removing fluoride too, which is another chemical added by some water sup-pliers. I'd suggest saving yourself the expense and only get a filter if you think that you have seriously gotten into fermenting. After all, it's not hard to leave some water out overnight if you are just mak-ing sauerkraut now and then. It's also noteworthy to mention that removing chemicals from your water is best practice. Having experimented a few times, I have noticed that my ferments will still work with chlorinated water, but the final product either doesn't taste quite as good or it takes a little longer to get going. The fact remains though, they still actually work. So again it comes down to personal choice.

A surprisingly easy and interesting alterna-tive to all of these methods is to add lemon juice at a 1:35 ratio (very approximately, this works out to 2 teaspoons [500 ml] per pint). This helps to neutral-

ize the chlorine *and* chloramine. This treatment can be a good option for brewers, as the ascorbic acid in the lemon also acts as a yeast nutrient. Interestingly, many of the older Norse (Viking) beer recipes call for juniper or spruce twigs to be added to water before brewing, as juniper contains antifungal and antimicrobial properties as well as ascorbic acid.

THE GOOD GUYS AND THE BAD GUYS

Fermenting is like panning for gold: Your aim is to rid yourself of the stuff you don't need and keep the good stuff. Rather than using a pan you use salt or sanitizer to sift out any unwanted guests. Good fermentation rewards you with foods rich in taste and nutrients, and bad fermentation can make you very ill. Luckily, most of the basic techniques are as easy to pick up as panning for gold.

Salt, yeast, and acid—and in some cases certain strains of mold—are in your arsenal when it comes to fermentation. They are what keep the bad guys out and the good guys in.

SALT AND ACID

Salt is one of your friends, as it helps kill off certain bacteria by effectively sucking all the moisture out of them. Luckily, not all bacteria are killed off by a bit of salt. The good guys, or the *Lactobacillus bacterium*, are salt tolerant, which means that as they are getting established in your jar they are being given a competitive edge.

Think of your fermentation jars like their own ecosystem. If you were growing vegetables in a garden, you might pull out all the weeds in order to favor your vegetables. This is what you are doing with the salt: You are essentially weeding out the bad bacteria in order to let the good guys flourish.

Once the lactobacillus are comfortable they will start to "eat" the lactose and other sugars and convert them into lactic acid. The lactic acid will also help kill off any harmful bacteria.

Many of the fermented foods described in this book need a brine solution. I tend to measure around 1 tablespoon of salt per 1 pint (500 ml) of water, which makes a 4 percent brine. Making it is easy: Boil ½ cup of the water and then stir in the salt. Top up the container with the rest of the unchlorinated or filtered cold water. This method means that you don't have to wait quite so long for your brine to be ready. For most cultures a level of 1½ to 5 percent of salt in your water is the perfect amount. This measurement is by weight.

ADDING CULTURES?

A market is evolving for laboratory-created cultures to add in with your ferments. In some cases, it is imperative that you have a culture to get you started. Kefir or kombucha are two very good examples. That said, I have successfully made kefir from store-bought kefir poured into milk. Starters for kefir and kombucha can be found through the community of various fermentation groups; look for public notices for fermenting workshops in classified ads, on social media, and in health food store noticeboards. If you don't find any there, you can conduct a search for commercial vendors online.

When it comes to making sauerkraut, dill pickles, or most of the other ferment recipes in this book I really don't see the point in purchasing cultures. It's a waste of your money unless you are really struggling to get started. The bacteria you are after is already present on the skins of fruit and vegetables, so save your money and spend your hard-earned cash on more jars (or a spare copy of this book)!

YOUR FERMENTATION SPOT

In many of the recipes I recommend leaving your ferment to do its stuff in your usual fermentation spot. This might change throughout the year depending on your abode. Ideally you are hoping for a spot that keeps to a fairly constant temperature. I have thermostatically controlled heating in our house and this keeps it at a temperature of 65 to 75°F (18 to 22°C), which is ideal for fermentation.

Your setup could vary greatly and it might be hard to keep a constant temperature in your kitchen. If this is the case, then make a study of all the rooms in your house. Get an accurate thermometer and go from room to room taking notes of the temperature. You may find that there is a spot that keeps a constant temperature. This could be in a crawl space, basement, or garage. If you still find that you are struggling, then I would suggest getting a small heater and/or fan and setting them up somewhere in your house.

WHEN IS YOUR FERMENTATION READY?

You'll notice that, for many of these recipes, I might say to ferment until ready or at least ready to go in the refrigerator. Depending on where you live, the time of year you are fermenting, and your own sense of taste, the amount of time needed can alter significantly. This is because the necessary microbes work faster in hotter weather and slower in colder temperatures. This can mean a difference of a few days to a few weeks for some fermentations.

To get a sense of when it might be ready, you first need to know if your fermentation has at least started to ferment. A few indicators will tell the tale. First, use your eyes and look for bubbles. They will be resting around the food or on top of the jar. In the case of cranberries they may even move the fruit to the top of your jar. Next, use your nose. Is there a sour vinegary smell? If so, that is good. It might smell like old drains, farts, or even rotten eggs—and believe it or not that is good too. However, severe rotten food smells are not so good. If you react to the smell with a cough, or even gag a little, you will need to discard your ferment. Over time you may even be able

to start telling when your ferment is ready by smell alone.

The last sense you should use is your taste. Just pop some in your mouth and taste it. Does it taste good with a bit of a tang? When you first start out I'd suggest leaving your vegetable ferments for longer than three days and trying them every day for up to three weeks. Keep a careful note of the temperature too. This way you'll start to get an idea of just how you like your fermentations to taste, and accordingly you can adjust the amount of time you leave them out of the refrigerator.

YEAST

Fermenting with yeast can be very easy or more complicated depending on what you are doing. When I first started brewing beer, yeast seemed like a very simple ingredient. I simply added some to the wort (unfermented beer), kept it at the right temperature, and it worked. As with anything, the more I looked into it the more complicated it became. In fact, yeast can make a massive difference to beer, wine, or Boza (page 184). Choose your yeast strains carefully and try to match them with the flavor profile you are after. If you are lucky enough to have a local homebrew store, they should be able to help you choose.

For wines, beers, and hard cider it is important to keep bacteria strains out; many of them will spoil your beer. I have had beer that tasted like goats' feet and nail polish remover, and I've sipped wine that had turned to a jelly-like substance. I have to say that none of them were pleasant experiences. This is why you need to sanitize when it comes to making beers, wine, or hard cider. Details about sanitizing will follow. Some beers can be brewed using bacteria strains, but I have focused on yeast beers in this book as they make up 99 percent of the beer drunk on this planet.

Other drinks, however, use a combination of yeasts and bacteria. For example, the kombucha "scoby" is a blend of bacteria and yeast (scoby is an acronym for "symbiotic culture of bacteria and yeast"); kefir is similarly made up of yeast and bacteria; and to make boza as authentically as possible, two types of yeast and a starter rich in bacteria are mixed all together. If you are already getting confused, don't worry too much. You can make delicious fermented foods and drinks without having any knowledge of what is going on at all. If you do wish to know more information, you can start by checking out the Further Reading suggestions on page 275.

Techniques for Fermented Drinks

This section is here to help you make drinks perfectly each time. It is possible to start riffing straight away by using the recipes for guidance rather than following them to the letter, but it is important that you read this section before you start making your drinks, as it should help you minimize any problems. I hope you'll pick up a thing or two from my years of

experience and perhaps not make some of the same mistakes that I have made over the years.

THE JOYS OF CLEANING AND STERILIZING

You should always sanitize the vessels you use for beverages that ferment using yeast. This is a step up from just cleaning, which should be sufficient for bacterial ferments. The reason for sanitizing is to inhibit bacterial growth and to favor yeast growth. Problems with beer, wine, and mead fermentation often arise because this important step has been ignored.

When cleaning carboys (demijohns) there always seems to be a stubborn bit of dirt hiding in a hard-to-reach spot. It is useful to use specially adapted brushes that you can buy from your local homebrew shop. Use these brushes to clean carboys as thoroughly as possible.

Once everything has been cleaned, give everything another check for any deposits. For really stubborn stains you can soak them overnight with a bleach solution at a ratio of 1 fluid ounce per 1 gallon, ensuring that you rinse afterward. Avoid using scented toilet bleach, and remember to keep this out of reach from children and animals and to wear gloves and something to protect your skin when using. Having had a bleach burn I can assure you they are very unpleasant! Rinse the burn thoroughly under a cold tap if this happens to you.

Another option is to use Star San, a product you can buy at most homebrew stores. At the risk of sounding like I work for them, using Star San revolutionized my brewing process. It's far easier to use than bleach or other sanitizers. Simply dilute as per instructions on the package and then ensure that the foam produced touches everything you are going to use. I fill my 5-gallon fermentation bucket and slosh around 3 or 4 quarts of the Star San solution. I then pour out the Star San and I'm done—there is no need to rinse.

When fermenting using bacterial strains, you don't have to be quite so thorough. It is important that your fermentation vessel and equipment are at least clean. My preference is to pass everything through the dishwasher cycle on as hot a setting as possible. This not only washes everything but it steams it. For larger vessels and for those people who don't have a dishwasher, then hot soapy water will do the trick. Be sure to rinse thoroughly as soap kills bacteria, which is why we use it! When washing equipment that will be used for yeast fermentation, avoid using wire brushes or anything too abrasive on plastic equipment or on things that will scratch. You don't want to create little pockets where bacteria can thrive.

BOTTLING

When making big batches of drinks I siphon the liquid off the lees (the sediment at the bottom of the fermentation vessel) into either a jug or another bottling bucket. To do this you'll need a siphoning tube, one end of which you hold just above the sediment; you then suck the other end until the liquid starts to flow and place it in the jug or bottling bucket. This simplifies the bottling process, as you don't have to keep stopping and starting the siphoning process once it has begun. Always leave a *ulage*, which is a small gap of air at the top of each bottle. Around 1 inch (2 to 3 cm) is ample.

CHAPTER 2

Foraged and Fermented

I first started to forage when I was seven or eight years old. I can remember going to the bottom of my parents' garden with my brother and harvesting some stinging nettles to make soup. The results were terrible, as we ignored the advice about only picking young nettle tops. I instead made soup with stringy old nettles and the soup tasted *gritty*.

Nevertheless, I found great joy in knowing I could supply my family with a dish that didn't really cost anything. I still get a kick from supplying my family with food that I've picked myself. Both of my children have been able to forage for wild foods such as edible flowers and berries since the age of two, and both of them are fully versed in our first rule of foraging: If you are not 100 percent sure about something, then always ask Daddy before eating it.

If you are new to foraging, then please don't be put off by the countless media stories about the dangers. Yes, if you get it wrong, then the consequences can be fatal. However, to give it some context, according to the AAPCC (American Association of Poison Control Centers), 13 people died from eating a poisonous plant or mushroom in the United States in 2016. Compare that to the 40 people a year who die after being struck by lightning, or the 450 a year who die falling out of bed, and the 13 people who die from vending machine–related deaths in the United States every year. I guess that means foraging is as dangerous as getting food from a vending machine—don't tip that vending machine, people!

Even so, I'm not suggesting that you should just go out and eat anything you find. I have been witness to many close calls, especially by people who get excited about foraging and try to eat anything they see. Just remember, be as clever as a two-year-

old child and only eat what you are sure of, and if in doubt ask an expert forager.

I strongly urge you to pick up a good field guide. There are plenty out there to choose from. My main advice is that you get a field guide that works for you. We are all different, have different levels of knowledge, and learn in different ways.

A novice forager might want to pick up a book that has botanical drawings in them, as these can make it easy to identify a plant. I'd avoid using ones with only photographs, because plants tend to be very variable depending on the conditions they grow in. Dandelion leaves, for example, can vary from an inch or so long to a couple of feet depending on how much light they are getting. Photos are also dependent on how good the photographer is—even I struggle to identify from some of the scrappy pictures I've seen!

You may also want to choose a book that covers your state. Many such field guides are published by the larger university presses and are pretty good. There are more general foraging books out there too, and these will help you identify many plants that are universally edible. These guides focus on some of the more common wild plants, which is a great way to start. Many online groups can also help you identify your wild food. Always get a second opinion and don't just trust the opinion of one person online.

By far the most enjoyable way to learn about wild food is to go on an organized foraging walk. These are often run by highly experienced individuals who have dedicated their lives to wild food. See the resources section at the back of this book for help in locating one in your area.

Once you know you are picking edible food and not poison there are a few other things to watch out for. I suggest you don't pick near roads, don't pick on old industrial sites, and try to avoid picking around the edges of farmers' fields. I avoid farms if I think they may have sprayed fertilizer or if I am not sure about ownership, as even rural roadsides can belong to someone, sometimes with a gun. On that note, you must also ensure that you are foraging in an area that is open to the public. If in doubt, try to seek out a local ranger and ask them. I have noticed that many local rangers now have their own social media accounts.

Some worry about dog urine on plants, which is fairly benign. I am more concerned about poo, as 30 percent of dogs in the United States carry the parasitic worm, *Toxocara canis*. An infection of this worm can lead to blindness. As a result, I don't pick from near the paths in my dog-walker-friendly local park, I wash stuff that comes from farther away from the paths, and if I think someone may have scooped up something the dog left behind from what I've picked, I leave it alone.

Like most people who forage, I am very aware of my impact on the environment. I only pick what is in abundance and I always leave some for the wildlife. A good simple rule to follow is if you can count three of something, then pick the third and leave the rest. If you always forage from the same area, you'll soon see if you are having a detrimental effect on the landscape.

This might all seem like a lot to take in and it may be enough to put you off foraging for life. Please don't fret. The fact of the matter is that successful foraging boils down to common sense. You might know your local area better than anyone, and perhaps even the other people who inhabit it. Once folks know you are foraging, they often show genuine interest rather than hostility and, more often than not, a bottle of wine or some other wonder from your larder placates even the most angry farmer or landowner.

Elderflower Scented Burdock Stems

YIELD: 1 pint (500 g) burdock stems   SUGGESTED JAR SIZE: 1 pint (500 g)
PREP TIME: 3 hours, including picking time   FERMENTATION TIME: 3 days

I've always loved the flavor and smell of roasted burdock root, but it can be a real effort to dig out. So when, around 15 years ago, I read somewhere that burdock leaves are edible, I duly tried one. It was foul, the most bitter thing, I think, I have ever tasted. A lot has happened since then and I decided to reconsider burdock. It turns out you can eat the stem of the burdock leaf and the flowering stem too. This has to be peeled in order to take off all the bitter tasting chemical that coats the burdock plant. I tried again and it was delicious, both cooked and raw.

Burdock leaves are said to look like elephant ears, and indeed some specimens can grow leaves that seem that big! Easily mistaken with poisonous wild rhubarb (so make sure you know what that looks like), burdock tends to favor field edges and disturbed soil next to pathways in woodlands.

The leaf stalks are purplish green. The plant grows over two or three years in a similar fashion to a thistle. First the basal (base) leaves will spread out and help to establish the root. These die back over the winter before growing again in the spring and sending up a central seed stem. You can snap this off in late spring and early summer, and the plant will recover and grow another. This is also the time to take off the leaves without fear of killing off the plant. I only take off two or three leaves from each plant to give the burdock a chance to recover. The easiest way to harvest the leaves is to slice them off with a knife, although this might have its problems depending on the laws and perceived threat of carrying a knife in your neighborhood. Use your common sense and a certain amount of discretion.

Coincidentally, the best time to pick the leaves is also when elderflower is in blossom, making this combination a seasonal delight. For advice on picking and identifying elderflower, see Alcoholic Elderflower "Champagne" on page 70. You can make this recipe without the elderflower if they are not in season or are hard to come by in your area, but I think the perfumed scent really lifts the ferment.

INGREDIENTS

1 cup (250 ml) filtered or unchlorinated cold water

1½ teaspoons sea salt

5 to 10 burdock leaf stems (6 oz; 170 g)

1 tablespoon fresh elderflowers

INSTRUCTIONS

1. Boil half a cup of the water and then stir in the salt. Top up with the rest of the cold water. Ensuring it is cool enough helps to keep the water at a useable temperature without having to wait for it to cool.

2. Once you have taken the burdock leaves off the stems measure them against your mason jar. They will need to be a ½ inch shorter than your jar. Cut all the stems to this size.

3. Detach the stems from the elderflowers and sprinkle the elderflowers into the bottom of your mason jar. Place the burdock stems, one by one, into your jar. They should stuff right in.

4. Top up with your brine, put a weight on, and leave in a warm spot and out of direct sunlight for at least three days.

5. Once fermented, transfer to the refrigerator. You will need to keep a weight on these to remove the elderflowers as they have a tendency to float to the surface, attracting mold.

6. Use within six months, although they should last for a lot longer.

Note: Burdock leaf stems can be a little stringy. To counter this, eat them as young as possible and slice into ¼-inch (1-cm) chunks.

Fizzy Dandelion Heads

YIELD: 1 pint (500 g) dandelion heads   SUGGESTED JAR SIZE: 1 pint (500 g)
PREP TIME: Up to 1 hour, including picking time   FERMENTATION TIME: 3 to 4 days

Also known as blowballs and face-clock, dandelions are native to the west and north of the Rocky Mountains although, thanks in part to European settlers, they have spread throughout the country. They are also present across most of the world except Greenland and Central Africa.

This recipe calls for the flowers, which appear pretty much year-round. However, the best time to pick them is in the early spring when they are more abundant. All parts of the plant are edible. The roots can be dug up and then eaten raw or roasted, or dried, ground down, and then made into a hot drink. The leaves are eaten across the globe and in some places they are even cultivated and used in a similar fashion to spinach.

Pick on a sunny spring morning. Don't pick too early in the day as you may miss the flowers—they don't open until the sun hits them!

INGREDIENTS

1 pint (2 to 3 oz; 70 g) dandelion flowers
1 cup (250 ml) filtered or unchlorinated cold water
1½ teaspoons sea salt

INSTRUCTIONS

1. After picking the dandelions, place them on a flat surface and allow any insects to move off. Pick out any dandelions that are starting to seed and then pull off any pieces of stem remaining.

2. Plop them into your jar, don't stuff them in too much.

3. Boil half a cup of the water and then stir in the salt. Top up with the rest of the cold water. Ensuring there is no steam and you can dip your finger in the water without discomfort, pour this water over the dandelion flowers.

4. Place a weight or water-filled zip-top bag over the top of the flowers. The flowers are quite buoyant and so the weight is pretty important in order to keep them below the waterline.

5. Leave to ferment, out of direct sunlight and in your usual fermentation spot, for three to four days. The cooler the place the longer fermentation will take. Once fermented, keep refrigerated and use within a month.

Wild Dandelion Spring-Chi

YIELD: 1 pint (500 g) spring-chi   SUGGESTED JAR SIZE: 1 pint (500 g)
PREP TIME: Up to 1 hour, including picking time   FERMENTATION TIME: 3 days

Although dandelion spring-chi calls for a set of specific ingredients, you really don't have to stick to the list, nor do you have to be too prescriptive about the weights or volume of the plant ingredients. This recipe is designed to serve as a guideline in order for you to make your own with what's around you. I happened to make it in the spring, hence the name; however, you could rename it summer-chi or fall-chi and make it using wild edibles that you find in that season. As with all foraging, just be sure you know what you are picking.

If you make this in the spring, I'd highly recommend sticking to the recipe and using dandelion greens. They are an excellent source of vitamins and minerals such as vitamin A, folate, vitamin K, vitamin C, calcium, and potassium. The fermenting process changes the greens, which enables your body to absorb more of this goodness than otherwise.

INGREDIENTS

8 ounces (225 g) ramps leaves (wild garlic) or any other edible green with toughish leaves

2 ounces (60 g) dandelion greens

1 tablespoon sea salt

½ ounce (15 g) ramps (wild garlic) flowers

1 ounce (30 g) dandelion flowers

3 magnolia buds (if available, see page 60 for picking tips)

1 red chili

1 cup (250 ml) filtered or unchlorinated water

INSTRUCTIONS

1. Cut the ramps and the dandelion greens into 1-inch (3-cm) squares, then place in an unbreakable bowl and cover them with the salt.

2. Pound them with the blunt end of a rolling pin or meat hammer until they release some of their juices. This should take around 10 minutes.

3. Toss in the flowers—the reason for omitting the wild garlic, dandelion, and magnolia flowers until this point is so that they still show a flash of color in the jar.

4. Cut off the stem from the chili and slice in half. If you want to reduce the heat of the chili but keep some of the taste, remember to scrape out the inner pith.

5. Puree the ramp stems and the chili in a food processor, then massage this paste into your leaves.

6. Stuff all the contents of the bowl into your jar and then top up with the filtered water.

7. Add your weight or water-filled zip-top bag, ensuring the contents of the jar remain below the waterline. Add a small piece of material over your jar to protect from airborne pests.

8. Leave to ferment, out of direct sunlight and in your usual fermentation spot, for three to four days. The cooler the place the longer fermentation will take.

9. Once fermented, keep refrigerated and use within a month.

Pink Peppercorn Wild Greens

YIELD: 1 quart wild greens   SUGGESTED JAR SIZE: 1 widemouthed quart (1L)
PREP TIME: 1 to 2 hours, including picking time (plus 12 hours soaking time)   FERMENTATION TIME: 1 week

When I asked my good forager friend Martin to suggest a recipe for this book he handed me a small jar and said, "Here you go." What I tasted was a blend of flavors that are longing to be served together. Needless to say, the one small jar was not enough and I had to make my own.

As with Wild Dandelion Spring-Chi (page 44), this recipe can be adapted to which plants you have growing around. Chickweed, yellow dock (in moderation), plantain (*Plantago major* and *Plantago lanceolata L.*), ground ivy, lambs quarters, and garlic mustard can all be used. However, each comes with its own flavor profile, and you should try them beforehand so you can get an idea of the flavor before you start your ferment. Of course, the flavor will change, but often it becomes an enhanced version of what it was. Remember then, if you don't like something before it has fermented, you certainly won't like it after it has been!

The pink peppercorns and juniper berries both add something to the texture as well as to the taste of this ferment. Each bite is accompanied by a sort of perfumed floral flavor.

INGREDIENTS

3 large handfuls wild greens (see headnote for ideas)

2 tablespoons sea salt

2 tablespoons pink peppercorns

1 tablespoon juniper berries

Up to 1 quart (1 L) filtered or unchlorinated water or 1 quart wild greens, juiced

1 currant leaf

INSTRUCTIONS

1. Place the wild greens into an unbreakable bowl and cover them with the salt.

2. Pound them with the blunt end of a rolling pin or meat hammer until they release some of their juices. This should take around 10 minutes.

3. You can place a plate over the top of your wild greens and leave them overnight, allowing the salt to draw out a lot of the moisture. It's not essential that you do this but it is good practice. The more juice that is extracted the less water you have to add.

4. Stir in the pink peppercorns and juniper berries, ensuring they are evenly distributed.

5. Stuff the contents of the bowl into your quart jar. Push down on the contents of the jar. If the juices don't rise over the greens even with weights, then you will need to top up the level of liquid, as the greens need to be fully submerged. You have two choices: You can you use either the filtered water or a very healthy alternative is to juice up 2 quarts of wild greens and use that instead. This will also help enhance the flavor.

6. Squeeze the currant leaf in against the side of your jar.

7. Cover and leave to ferment, out of direct sunlight and in your usual fermentation spot, for up to a week. The cooler the place the longer fermentation will take.

8. Once fermented, keep refrigerated. They are best used within a month, although in all probability they will last for much longer.

Wild Mustard Greens

YIELD: 4 fluid ounces (120 ml) mustard greens
SUGGESTED JAR SIZE: ½ pint (250 ml) if available, 1 pint (500 ml) if not
PREP TIME: 1 hour, including picking time (plus 12 hours soaking time)   FERMENTATION TIME: 3 to 7 days

Wild mustard is a form of wild cabbage that was introduced to the United States, where it has spread to every state and is now classified as a weed. It also grows across much of Europe and Asia.

Wild mustard seeds are prized, and you'll find them in many recipes in this book. However, the leaves are often overlooked, which is a shame as they can liven up many dishes and are very easy to forage. I chop them up and add them to soups and stews, or I tear out any woody stems and use them to spice up a salad. They can also be added to a sandwich or burger.

Mustard grows in the cracks of sidewalks, in field margins, and on the edges of woodlands. Look for the tiny little yellow flowers with four petals in a cross. The jagged leaves first grow at the base rather like a thistle or dandelion,

then a central stem grows, containing many flowers. Pick the plant just before it flowers if possible and then tear off the leaves. The stems can get quite woody, so discard any that feel like twigs. It's possible to confuse wild mustard with ragweed, which is very poisonous, so if you are unsure get a good wild plant guide.

This recipe is simplicity itself and creates a kraut with a kick! Serve as you would a regular mustard condiment. I have also chosen to keep this recipe small, as I find it best used as a condiment and not as food in its own right. However, that is my personal choice and there is nothing to stop you from increasing the amount of ingredients in this recipe—you could start by adding other herbs and spices to enhance the flavor, perhaps even some mustard seeds. You could also make this recipe using different wild cabbage plants—all are edible.

INGREDIENTS

4 ounces (120 g) mustard leaves

1 teaspoon sea salt

2 cups (500 ml) filtered or unchlorinated water

INSTRUCTIONS

1. Cut the mustard greens into small pieces, then place in an unbreakable bowl. Sprinkle the salt over and then pound it with a meat hammer. You are aiming to break the cellulose structure of the mustard.

2. Place a small plate over the bowl of mustard greens and leave overnight.

3. Transfer the mustard greens to a jar and then top up with the water. Place a weight over the mustard leaves and ensure they stay below the waterline as this helps prevent mold growth.

4. Cover with an airlock or a small piece of material and leave in your usual fermentation spot out of direct sunlight to ferment.

5. Check the taste of your ferment after three days. If it is to your level of sourness, then refrigerate and use within six months. You may wish to leave for a little longer before refrigerating. Anything up to around two weeks is fine.

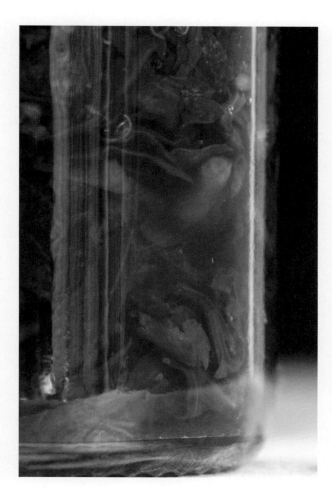

Fermented Pine Needle "Tea"

YIELD: 1 quart (1 L) tea   SUGGESTED JAR SIZE: 1 quart (1 L)
PREP TIME: 5 minutes   FERMENTATION TIME: 5 days to 2 weeks, depending on room temperature

This is a simple recipe that is thought to have originated in ancient China before finding its way to the Korean peninsula where it goes by various names according to which pine is used.

To make authentic *sollip-cha* you must use needles from the Korean red pine or the Manchurian red pine *P. tabuliforme*; if made from Korean pine (*P. koraiensis*), it is known as *jannip-cha*. Originally this tea was made using honey, but it works equally well with sugar. You're unlikely to find Korean pines anywhere outside Asia, though you may come across them in yards and gardens.

You can use any true pine needles, apart from yellow pine, to make this tea. I've successfully made this tea using Scots pine, the most common pine in the world. Eastern white pine *P. strobus* also comes recommended.

Make sure you are not using yew pine (*Podocarpus macrophyllus*) or Norfolk Island pine (*Araucaria heterophylla*), which are not true pines. Both are poisonous. There is some speculation that yellow pine, also known as Ponderosa Pine, could be harmful, at least to cattle. Pregnant women should avoid all pine needle tea. Please refer to the foraging tips on page 6, and, remember, do not use anything you find foraging as an ingredient unless you are absolutely sure it is okay to ingest.

The taste isn't too dissimilar to root beer and I find that when drinking this tea, the taste of pine still lingers a little while after consumption and is most refreshing. You'll also notice that the pine flavor is greater or lesser depending on the season you pick your needles. In the winter months you may need to add many more pine needles to get a good strong flavor.

Pine can clear the sinuses, and for this reason I like to give pine needle tea to my family when there are coughs and colds going around to help ease their breathing.

INGREDIENTS
3¾ cups (850 ml) filtered or unchlorinated water
4 ounces (120 g) honey or sugar
4 ounces (120 g) pine needles

INSTRUCTIONS

1. Boil the water before stirring in the honey and then stir until fully dissolved. Allow to cool.

2. Cut the sharp points and the woody ends from the pine needles and place inside your jar. Pour the water solution over the needles and leave in a warmish spot in sunlight. Cover with a piece of material or a tea towel to keep out any dust or flies.

3. After five days, a few bubbles will start to form on the top and around the needles and at this point it is ready to drink, although I leave mine for a little bit longer to make a drier drink.

4. Once it has brewed to your satisfaction, it can be refrigerated and drunk within a month or so. You will need to vent the gas now and then, as your pine needle tea will continue to ferment.

5. Once ready, it is consumed cold and served diluted like a cordial. I like mine at a ratio of 2:1, although you can dilute it further to taste depending on how sweet you like your *sollip-cha*.

Blackberry Leaf Tea

YIELD: 4 ounces (120 g) tea   SUGGESTED JAR SIZE: 1 pint (500 ml)
PREP TIME: 1 hour, including plenty of time to pick   FERMENTATION TIME: 6 weeks

Sometimes when you are out foraging it is hard to get a real abundance of a product; not so with this next recipe. If there are blackberries growing in your neighborhood, then you can be sure they will be spreading. Many people even classify this delicious fruit as a weed, and it has been said that the thorns are like lawyers, once they hook you in you can't get out. When picking from the wild, I prefer to pick from many different plants, as I believe the greater diversity improves the flavor of the tea, and also ensures that you are not decimating a habitat for local invertebrates. Go for the top leaves, leaving the coarse, harder leaves behind.

I recommend wearing gloves while you pick these leaves as they can have quite a few spikes hiding on the leaf stems. The braver among you will soon realize that a delicate but firm pinch-and-pull technique will quickly furnish

a basketful of leaves to turn into tea. Ideally, I'd pick in the early spring as the leaves tend to get a little thicker later in the season. If you are trying to visualize what 4 ounces (100 g) of blackberry leaves look like, imagine an adult-size baseball cap, or a bowler hat if you are from the UK.

INGREDIENTS

4 ounces (120 g) blackberry leaves

INSTRUCTIONS

1. Empty the leaves out onto the countertop. With your meat hammer or rolling pin bash the leaves. You are trying to break the cell structure to encourage fermentation. After about five minutes of pulverizing, your leaves will be ready.

2. Being careful not to be pricked, place the leaves into a jar. Around 4 ounces will neatly fit inside a pint-sized mason jar. Seal tightly.

3. Leave for six weeks in a warm place and out of direct sunlight. I find that the leaves can develop a furry mold after a week or so. To help prevent this, sporadically take the leaves out of the jar and pull them apart. If you do see a furry mold, you must throw the whole thing out.

4. After two or three weeks they will start to darken and the aroma will change; it becomes rather sweet smelling and "of the forest." Some say it smells more powerfully of blackberries, but I am not sure if this is the best way to describe the aroma; it certainly smells more like the fall.

5. The next step is to process them—they will need to be dry. To do this you can either turn your oven on to a low heat of around 200°F (100°C) with the door open a little or pop them into a dehydrator. In both cases keep them in there until they are dry to the touch. The time will vary in accordance to how dry the leaves are when you put them in.

6. Once dry, put on your gloves and rub the leaves until they crumble into small flakes. Or you can also pass them through a wire sieve, but it's much less fun.

7. Store your leaves in a dark, airtight container.

8. To make the tea, use 1 teaspoon of blackberry leaves per cup of hot water and leave it to steep for a little longer than regular black tea—about five minutes.

Note: You could take a (tea) leaf out of the book of Sweden where these leaves are mixed with regular black tea to make a fragrant and uplifting tea to rival Earl Grey. I recommend a 3:1 mix for something fruity but not overpowering.

Fermented Spiny Sow Thistle and Dandelion Stems with Turmeric and Celery

YIELD: 1 quart (1 L) stems   SUGGESTED JAR SIZE: 1 quart (1 L)
PREP TIME: 2 hours, including 1½ hours foraging time, 30 minutes prep   FERMENTATION TIME: 3 days

The spiny sow thistle was introduced to America from its native Europe. It has now taken hold in every state, a fact that might anger golf course owners but should delight foragers, as it is full of vitamins and minerals such as calcium, phosphorous, iron, and vitamins A, B1, B2, B3, and C.

I've found sow thistle growing in most habitats. I even found a 6-foot-tall specimen hiding behind a tree in the garden of a friend who prided herself in ridding her lawn of weeds. I've also seen one growing out of a pocket of dirt on a palm tree. Check forest edges, unkept fields, cracks in pavements, meadows, parks, gardens, and palm trees. Dandelions grow in similar habitats too. See the recipe for Fizzy Dandelion Heads (page 42) for more details.

The dandelion and spiny sow thistle both have a diuretic effect on your system. This means that they help you flush out salt. They may have many other health benefits, such as helping to reduce blood pressure.

The addition of turmeric completes this ferment and gives it quite an earthy flavor, which, when coupled with the freshness from the sow thistle, leaves you wanting more.

INGREDIENTS

3 ounces (90 g) dandelion leaves
3 ounces (90 g) spiny sow thistle leaves
1 ounce (30 g) fresh turmeric or ginger, grated
4 to 5 sticks of celery
2 cups (500 ml) filtered or unchlorinated cold water
1 to 2 tablespoons sea salt

INSTRUCTIONS

1. Rinse the dandelion and sow thistle leaves and then cut off the stems to be set aside. You can also tear out the stem—it won't be so neat but is rather satisfying.

2. Grate the turmeric. I wear gloves for this job. If you don't, it can dye your hands yellow and make it look like you smoke 60 cigarettes a day.

3. Slice the celery and stems into strips. The length will be dictated by the height of your 1-quart jar. Put your jar on its side and line them up lengthwise to get the measure right. You can munch on the cut-off stems or add them to your next sauerkraut to give it a little bite (see page 136).

4. Put half of the stems in the jar, add the grated turmeric, and then stuff in the dandelion and sow thistle leaves, celery, and remaining stems. You shouldn't be able to fit in any more. Aim to wedge them tightly.

5. Boil a little of the water, stir in the salt, and top up with the rest of the cold water, ensuring that it is at least cooler than room temperature, and pour into your jar, covering the stems. If the stems are stuffed in tightly enough, they will not move and you may not need to weigh them down.

6. Put a piece of material or a tea towel over your jar to keep out bugs and leave in your usual fermentation spot.

7. After three to four days place in the refrigerator and use within three months.

Rosehip and Horseradish Sauce

YIELD: 12 ounces (360 ml) horseradish sauce
SUGGESTED JAR SIZE: 12 ounce (360 ml) if available, 1 pint (500 ml) if not
PREP TIME: 2 to 3 hours   FERMENTATION TIME: 2 to 5 days

The best horseradish roots can be found across most of the United States, apart from the southern states, in the fall. This is a good time to find them in Europe and western Asia too. Luckily, this is also the same time that rosehips are in abundance, as they go so well together. I have seen horseradish roots take over scraps of land. This is because horseradish will grow from the tiniest piece of root left in the soil. This also means you can harvest without worrying about decimating the population and, what's more, once you have found a source it should return year after year. Horseradish tends to grow on scraps of land and across wasteland, especially across former homesteads. Grating the horse-radish is a great job if you have a cold or sinus trouble. It's not so good in a confined space or if you are sensitive to smells. Depending on your

tolerance level you may wish to wear goggles, as it can make the eyes stream somewhat. You may also want to wear something to protect your nostrils such as a surgical mask.

If you can't find any growing near your neighborhood, search for it in specialty grocery stores or put a shout-out across social media.

This recipe also asks for deseeded rosehips, which can be a chore. From experience, the bigger rosehips such as the ones from the dog rose (*Rosa canina*) are easier to deseed than much smaller ones. Deseeding can be a messy and itchy job, and I keep a bowl of water handy so that I can dip my fingers and clean them between each rosehip. I also use a small knife and scrape out the seeds. It's this job that makes the prep time so long for this recipe.

This recipe might not seem like a bed of roses to prepare, and I am sure it sounds worse on paper than it actually is. However, I think you will be really pleased with the results. It is one of those recipes that never fails to get a wow when it is eaten. Serve with lamb, game, and other rich meats.

INGREDIENTS

1 cup grated horseradish
½ cup deseeded rosehips
½ cup (125 ml) filtered or unchlorinated water
1 teaspoon sea salt
1 tablespoon liquid from a previous ferment (if available)
1 teaspoon apple cider vinegar
1 teaspoon honey
1 teaspoon black mustard seeds (optional)

INSTRUCTIONS

1. Layer the inside of your jar with one layer of grated horseradish root, then cover with rosehips. Repeat the process until you get to the top of the jar. You can add more rosehips if you wish for a lighter sauce.

2. Boil a small amount of the water. Stir in the salt and cook until it is fully dissolved, then top up with the rest of the cold water.

3. Pour the brine into the jar. Add the liquid from your previous ferment if available. Weigh down the solids. Cover with a small piece of material or tea towel to keep out any airborne pests.

4. Leave for three to five days, ensuring that it begins to bubble within this time.

5. Once it has fermented, gently pour out most of the liquid. You'll need to retain a little to help the food processor do its job—you can use the excess liquid for another fermentation or to start another batch of sauce.

6. Scoop out the contents of the jar and place them into a blender with a small amount of the water and blend until a rough paste forms. Stir in the vinegar and honey. I also like to stir in a teaspoon of black mustard seeds to give a little crunch.

7. Keep refrigerated and use within six months.

Spring Flower Tang

YIELD: 1 quart (1 L) tang   SUGGESTED JAR SIZE: 1 quart (1 L)
PREP TIME: 20 to 30 minutes   FERMENTATION TIME: 3 to 5 days

The inspiration for this recipe comes from the Korean staple, Kimchi (page 116). I decided that I could do away with some of the traditional ingredients and still have something that is close to the original, at least in flavor. Conventional garlic can be replaced with ramsons (ramps or wild garlic), and there are hints of ginger in the magnolia buds. I also threw in some primroses too, really just for an extra splash of color. Yet the magnolia buds are the chief ingredient. Magnolia buds are similar to ginger, but think of the strongest ginger you have ever tasted and you will start to come close. In other words they are bursting with spice. There is also a hint of pepper, an earthiness, and a floral note too—indeed I have heard them described as rose petals on steroids. To get to know magnolia buds better, try fermenting them on their own (see Cultured Magnolia Buds on page 60).

This recipe can be the basis for a bit of experimentation. Try swapping the traditional Napa cabbage for some wild cabbage, swap the magnolia for rose petals, or add wild leeks instead of wild garlic. The wild world is your oyster—or should that be your kimchi.

Be careful when picking ramsons (wild garlic) as they come up at the same time as some other poisonous look-alikes, such as *Arum italicum Mill* (Italian lords and ladies). When picking magnolia be sure to pick just the buds before they open out. Please refer to the foraging tips on page 6, and, remember, do not use anything you find foraging as an ingredient unless you are absolutely sure it is okay to ingest.

INGREDIENTS

1 Napa cabbage (or equivalent amount of wild cabbage leaves)

1 grated carrot

3 ounces (90 g) ramps (wild garlic)

10 magnolia buds

½ pint primroses

½ teaspoon chili flakes

1 tablespoon sea salt

4 tablespoons liquid from a previous ferment (if available)

INSTRUCTIONS

1. Slice the hard bottom off the cabbage and compost. Cut the cabbage into four, then slice into ribbons. The ends are a bit thicker but can still be sliced up finely too and added; treat them as you would onions. Chuck into a large unbreakable bowl. Add the carrot.

2. Cut the ramps into ½- to 1-inch pieces.

3. Take off any hard, green, furry leaves covering the magnolia buds. Slice off the bottom bits and then scatter the leaves into the bowl. Take out the stamen and put them to one side. Add the rest of the ingredients.

4. Start pounding; this should be done firmly but gently with a meat hammer until you start to see liquid forming at the bottom of the bowl. This should take around 10 minutes.

5. You can now start stacking it into your quart jar. I like to sprinkle in the magnolia stamen one by one at this point, so they run up the inside of the jar. The reason I leave them out up to this point is partly aesthetic, as I find them so beautiful that I want them to stay intact but also partly due to the taste. They are like an intense little burst that explodes in your mouth as you eat—you need to try it to understand.

6. Push the ferment down inside the jar and weigh down the ingredients so that the waterline stays above anything solid.

7. Cover loosely and leave out of direct sunlight for three to five days, and then refrigerate. Use within three months.

Cultured Magnolia Buds

YIELD: 8 ounces (250 ml) magnolia buds
SUGGESTED JAR SIZE: 8 ounce (250 ml) if available, 1 pint (500 ml) if not
PREP TIME: 5 minutes, plus 20 minutes foraging time   FERMENTATION TIME: 3 days

It seemed a shame not to give magnolia buds their own fermenting jar and so I did. These can be added to stews or used in place of relish when you are eating burgers or other greasy meats, as they help cut through the fat and enhance the meat flavors. They are also a colorful addition to salads.

When picking magnolia make sure you get the right species. You should avoid a sub-species of big leaf magnolia called *Magnolia macrophylla subsp. ashei* that grows in the southeastern states. It is considered endangered and, what's more, I can't find any references to its edibility. Instead, head for *Magnolia grandiflora*. This magnolia is native to the south-western Atlantic states but is often cultivated throughout the United States except in those locations that experience hard freezes. They are prized for their flowers, so please don't sneak into someone's yard to pick them. At least ask first. The part you are going for is the bud, and this should be picked just before the flower opens out.

INGREDIENTS

1 cup (250 ml) filtered or unchlorinated water
1½ teaspoons sea salt
14 magnolia buds
1 inch (3 cm) lemon zest

INSTRUCTIONS

1. Make the brine by boiling the water and adding the salt. Allow to cool.

2. Peel any outer hard protective (furry) leaves from the outside of the bud. Cut off the bottoms of the bud and then add the petals one by one into your jar before adding the lemon zest.

4. Pour over the cooled brine, add the weight, cover, and place in a warm spot out of direct sunlight to ferment.

5. Leave for three days, then transfer to the refrigerator and use within one month.

Pickled Pine Buds

YIELD: 12 ounces (360 ml) pine buds
SUGGESTED JAR SIZE: 12 ounce (360 ml) if available, 1 pint (500 ml) if not
PREP TIME: 1 hour, including picking time   FERMENTATION TIME: 2 days

Around the middle to the end of spring, lots of people start to sneeze, have watery eyes, and dry coughs. Many might attribute this to the last vestige of the winter cold season, but more likely these are symptoms of an allergy or hay fever triggered by pine pollen.

The air can be thick with these big particles, and when mixed with a bit of pollution they can make your life a misery. If you knock past a pine tree, you might see plumes of yellow pollen filling the air. Every tree seems to make an abundance of it. When I realize what is going on I start to drink more nettle and elderflower tea to counter the symptoms. However, there is a really positive side to all that pine pollen, and it is the pine buds. They are delicious—especially when fermented.

For notes on poisonous species, look-alikes, and identification of pine trees, see the recipe for Fermented Pine Needle "Tea" (page 50). Please refer to the foraging tips on page 6, and, remember, do not use anything you find foraging as an ingredient unless you are absolutely sure it is okay to ingest.

The pine buds have a short season. Forage too early and there won't be any on the tree; forage too late and they will have expelled all their pollen. Spent pine buds resemble shriveled-up little paperlike finger shapes on the tree. Ideally, you will collect little solid yellow-green, egg-shaped buds. They grow in clusters at the base of the needles. Try to catch them when they are this color and solid. This is usually about a month into the spring, or when everyone starts to complain about hay fever. You can pick a little later in the season too, because not all pine trees start producing pollen at the same time. I forage on a fairly big hill and often the picking season is different on the top than it is on the bottom. If you just miss the season, you might be okay: Pine buds are usable just about when they start to turn, so long as one or two in the cluster are still fairly solid.

To pick the pine buds, grip the whole bud in your fist and twist it off the tree. It should be easy enough to find some at ground level; you shouldn't need to climb the tree. I like to collect mine straight into the jar that I am going to ferment them in. This ensures that none of that lovely pollen goes to waste. Be careful to pull off any dead buds or needles. Also, try not to trap any insects in the jar. When in doubt, you can leave the jar on its side when you get home so that the insects have time to escape.

Fermented pine buds can be eaten as a little snack or can be added to salads to give them an unusual bite. It is said that pine buds can help you produce testosterone and therefore act as a libido enhancer. They are also said to help balance moods and to promote DNA repair.

INGREDIENTS

1 cup (250 ml) filtered or unchlorinated water
1½ teaspoons sea salt
2 ounces (60 g) pine buds

INSTRUCTIONS

1. Make up the brine by boiling a small amount of the water and stirring in the sea salt until it is dissolved. Top up with the rest of the water.

2. Ensuring your brine is at room temperature, pour it over the buds in the jar. Add a weight if necessary to ensure that the buds stay below the waterline.

3. Cover with an airlock or a small piece of material and leave in your usual fermentation spot out of direct sunlight to ferment.

4. After two days, move the jar to the refrigerator and use within two months.

Pickled Ribes (Currant) Blossoms

YIELD: 1 pint (500 ml) currant blossoms   SUGGESTED JAR SIZE: 1 pint (500 ml)
PREP TIME: 30 minutes, including picking time   FERMENTATION TIME: 3 days

Both native and introduced, the blackcurrant or *Ribes nigram L.* can be found across the United States and Europe. Look for small bushes up to 5 feet (1.5 m) tall. The plant has maplelike leaves that are small at the blossom stage. Often these bushes are planted at the edges of parks and in ornamental gardens where nonfruiting varieties are often grown.

Gather the blossoms in early spring, remembering to leave a few for the bees. Pick the blossoms on a hot sunny day, in the morning if possible as the nectar will be at the highest. If you are certain you are picking the right plant, then you can have a taste of the blossoms there and then. Ideally you are looking for a blackcurrant taste with a bit of background bitterness.

Once fermented, the blossoms can be used in a variety of dishes. My favorite is toffee ice cream with a few fresh basil leaves. But they also work very well with savory dishes and especially on meats such as lamb, venison, and duck.

INGREDIENTS

1 cup (250 ml) filtered or unchlorinated water

1 teaspoon sea salt

2 cups (2.2 oz; 65 g) ribes blossoms

2 or 3 small ribes leaves

INSTRUCTIONS

1. Make up the brine by boiling the water, stirring in the salt until it is dissolved, and then allowing it to cool.

2. Pack the blossoms into your jar, adding a leaf or two from the bush you picked from. This adds a little bit of astringency and bite and also deepens the flavor.

3. Pour over the brine and add the weight or water-filled zip-top bag. The blossoms will rise up in the jar, so it is important to keep a saucer under your jar; otherwise, I find quite a puddle after making these!

4. Place in a warm spot out of direct sunlight and leave for three days.

5. Refrigerate and use within a few months—although they should keep for up to a year.

Fermented Stinging Nettle Paste

YIELD: 1 pint (500 ml) nettle paste   SUGGESTED JAR SIZE: 1 pint (500 ml)
PREP TIME: 1 hour, including foraging time (plus 24 to 36 hours soaking time)   FERMENTATION TIME: 10 to 14 days

There are two type of nettles in the United Statets that get confused with each other. They are the stinging nettle (*Urtica dioica*) and the wood nettle (*Laportea canadensis*). The wood nettle lives in partial shade along river bottoms, and it has oval-shaped leaves that grow rather like maritime pine, which is to say the foliage is bigger and more concentrated at the top of the plant. The stinging nettle lives in full sun, and its leaves are the same size sitting opposite each other all the way up the plant. I have yet to ferment wood nettle, but I suspect their stems are delicious when picked in the spring and fermented. Be careful when you work with wood nettle, as its sting can pack quite a punch.

The best time to pick a proper stinging nettle is during the springtime when they are young and full of an earthy richness. Later in the season they build up a certain amount of

uric acid, which can be harmful, not to mention that it crystallizes in the plant, which can make you feel like you are eating sand.

Picking the nettles is best done with a pair of scissors and a bowl or basket to catch them in. Alternatively, you can wear gloves and pick them by hand. Pick the top four leaves of the plant. This is for two reasons: First, they are the best and tastiest leaves and, second, the plant will recover and grow two *heads* in place of the one you picked.

Nettles are rich in vitamin K, a vitamin that helps to remove lactic acid. I suspect this is why your nettles need some culture from a previous ferment in order to get started. Please note that nettles can cause a serious skin irritation, so wear gloves whenever you handle them.

INGREDIENTS

5 cups (1 oz, 28g) nettles

1 tablespoon sea salt

3 tablespoons liquid from a previous ferment

½ cup (125 ml) filtered or unchlorinated water or nettle juice

INSTRUCTIONS

1. Cut the nettle leaves into ½-inch pieces and place into a large bowl.

2. Sprinkle with the salt and leave for 24 to 36 hours. This will help wilt the tiny hairs that sting you. If you find you are still getting a bit of a sting when taking the nettles out of the bowl, leave for a little longer until all the tiny hairs have wilted.

3. Pack the nettles into your fermentation jar and ensure that you pour any moisture collected in your bowl in with the nettles.

4. Add the 3 tablespoons liquid from a previous ferment.

5. Observe the waterline of the nettles; if the water doesn't cover them, add some to all of the filtered water.

6. Add a weight to the nettles, cover with a small piece of material or airlock, and leave to ferment out of direct sunlight for at least 10 days or until it changes from green to more of a rusty color.

7. Taste test the nettles and if they are to your liking, refrigerate and use within three months.

Ramp and Wild Mustard Seed Mustard

YIELD: ½ pint (250 ml) mustard   SUGGESTED JAR SIZE: ½ pint (250 ml)
PREP TIME: 10 minutes   FERMENTATION TIME: 3 to 4 days

There is something truly delicious about combining mustard and garlic. However, mustard seeds often come into season long after the ramps have died back. This means you either have to cheat a little and use store-bought mustard seeds or keep some back from the previous season's harvest.

The seeds from ramps come into season around midsummer in most states. The leaves die off leaving the central seed stem in the shape of a lollipop that's covered in small clusters of seedpods. The seeds sit inside these pods and, when fully ripe, are easily obtained with a little shake or rub.

Both yellow and black mustard seeds can be used in this recipe, but you are more likely to find black mustard seeds in the wild. For more on wild mustard, including where to forage and identification tips, see the recipe for Wild Mustard Greens (page 48). For more information on ramps (wild garlic), see the recipe for Spring Flower Tang (page 58). Yellow mustard is actually native to the United States, but it (mostly) only grows in a few counties in California.

INGREDIENTS

4 ounces (120 g) wild (if possible) yellow or black mustard seeds

4 ounces (120 g) bold ramp seeds

1 cup (250 ml) filtered or unchlorinated water

¾ cup raw apple cider vinegar

1 tablespoon sea salt

INSTRUCTIONS

1. Place all the ingredients into a ½-pint (500-ml) jar and stir well. I like to use a wooden chopstick for stirring ferments such as this one as it helps to pinpoint the rogue mustard or garlic seeds that stick to the side of the jar. Although I like to steer clear of plastic at any given opportunity, I would also advise placing a water-filled zip-top bag over the top of this ferment. And try as you might, there will always be a few mustard seeds above the waterline. If you have an airlock, then using that will certainly have the same effect.

2. Cover your jar with a small piece of material.

3. Leave the jar in a cool, dark spot for three days.

4. Once fermented, you can transfer into smaller jars and give away as presents. Remember to keep refrigerated and use within a year or so.

Alcoholic Elderflower "Champagne"

YIELD: 1 gallon (4 L) "champagne"   **SUGGESTED FERMENTATION VESSEL:** Fermentation bin, 1-gallon (4-L) carboy
PREP TIME: 4 hours (spread out over the course of a few days)
MINIMUM FERMENTATION TIME: 10 days and an additional 3 months

This recipe was developed over a number of years. It came about due to the high volume of e-mails I received from people who struggled to make elderflower champagne the traditional way (see page 76 for Not-So-Alcoholic Wild Yeast Elderflower "Champagne"). I wanted a recipe that took away the margin of error and created a product that didn't rely so much on wild yeast and that wasn't so prone to exploding in the bottle. The following process owes much to the sparkling winemaking process that I learned about after visiting Roberto Bava at the Bava winery in northern Italy. It's not a recipe for the beginner, unless you are feeling brave and have eliminated the explosive nature of the final product by using thick champagne bottles. Please do not use thin glass bottles when making this, as it could be dangerous. (See the discussion in the Author's Note on page 7 about the possibility of exploding bottles.)

Speaking of danger, not all elder trees are equal. You are safe using the flower and fruit from the American black elder (*Sambucus canadensis*). Just don't eat the berries raw. This elder grows throughout the American Midwest, the East Coast, and California. Those living in Washington, Colorado, most of North and South Dakota, Utah, most of Texas, Idaho, Nevada, and Europe should be able to find the black elder (*Sambucus nigra*). Again this is fine to use as long as you don't eat the berries raw. However, there are some poisonous varieties of elder, so you really need to be certain that you are picking from the correct elder. Familiarize yourself with the American red elder (*Sambucus pubens*) and the European dwarf elder (*Sambucus ebulus*) so that you can avoid them, as both will cause you serious trouble. Please refer to the foraging tips on page 6, and, remember, do not use anything you find foraging as an ingredient unless you are absolutely sure it is okay to ingest.

Elder grows in wastelands and on field edges. The seeds are spread by birds, so if left unattended the trees will pop up in almost any scrap of uncultivated land.

I tend to pick whole clusters of elderflower, placing them lightly on top of each other in a basket. A 2-gallon (9-L) basketful will be plenty enough to make wine. Don't drink the raw juice of the berries as it is poisonous. Also, be sure to remove the flowers completely from the stem as the wood contains cyanide. Your body can tolerate small amounts of cyanide, so you don't have to be overly zealous, but you don't want to take any chances of an adverse reaction. Besides, too many woody stems will taint the wine.

continued

INGREDIENTS

6 pounds (3 kg) sugar, plus 2 ounces (60 g) for final fermentation

8 pints (3.5 L) boiling water, plus 1 cup (250 ml) for final fermentation

2 pints (1 L) of elderflowers

Zest of one lemon

Juice of five lemons

One ½-ounce (15-g) packet champagne yeast

1 teaspoon yeast nutrient

1 pint (500 ml) white grape juice concentrate

INSTRUCTIONS

1. While you sterilize your fermentation vessel, leave the elderflowers on some dry paper for a couple of hours to allow any insects to leave home.

2. Mix the 6 pounds sugar and the 8 pints boiling water in a large pan.

3. Using a fork, pull off all the flowers from the elderflower clusters and let them drop into your fermentation vessel.

4. Drop in the zest and lemon juice.

5. Pour over the still hot sugar solution and leave to cool to around 68°F (20°C).

6. Filter through a cheesecloth, then pitch (add) the champagne yeast and yeast nutrient. Leave in a place with a steady temperature of around 68°F (20°C) for 10 days. After this time most of the primary fermentation will have ceased.

7. Strain into a carboy or demijohn and allow to ferment fully. About three months should do the job. Keep checking with a hydrometer, and when you get consistent, stable readings over three to four days your wine will have fully fermented.

8. Bring 1 cup (250 ml) of water to a boil and add 2 ounces (70 g) of sugar. Allow cooling, then strain the wine into another demijohn, leaving the sediment. Add the sugar solution to the demijohn and leave in a warm place for 24 hours. This part of the process introduces enough sugar to restart the fermentation just enough to create some bubbles.

9. Siphon into champagne bottles, seal with champagne corks, and secure them in place with metal cages. The wine should be kept at room temp for the first 10 days, then moved to a cooler place, such as a cellar—ideally it will need to be stored at 53°F (12°C).

10. Initially the bottles should be stored horizontally, and over the next three months they should be gradually moved upside down. This can be done by placing the neck into damp sand. Chill for 24 hours before serving and do not disturb the bottle before opening.

Note: *I recommend that you age your champagne for a year before drinking, if you can bear the wait. Theoretically, it should keep for a number of years, but I have yet to keep a bottle unopened for that long!*

Elderberry Wine

YIELD: 1 gallon (4.5 L) wine   SUGGESTED FERMENTATION VESSEL: Fermentation bin, 1-gallon (4-L) carboy

PREP TIME: 2 hours   MINIMUM FERMENTATION TIME: 3 to 4 days and an additional 1 month

When picking elderberries you need to be certain that you are picking from the correct elder.

The American red elder (*Sambucus pubens*) and the European dwarf elder (*Sambucus ebulus*) are the wrong type of elders. The berries from these elders are poisonous enough to kill you. Instead, when foraging in the wild, look for the American black elder (*Sambucus canadensis*), which grows throughout the American Midwest, the East Coast, and California. Those living in Washington, Colorado, most of North and South Dakota, Utah, most of Texas, Idaho, Nevada, and Europe should be able to find the black elderberry (*Sambucus nigra*). Again, do not eat the berries raw.

Elder grows in wastelands and on field edges. The seeds are spread by birds, so if left unattended the trees will pop up in almost any scrap of uncultivated land.

I tend to pick whole clusters of elderberries, placing them lightly on top of each other in a basket. A 2-gallon basketful will be plenty enough to make wine. Don't drink the raw juice of the berries as it is poisonous. Also, be sure to remove the berries completely from the stem, as the wood contains cyanide. Small amounts can be tolerated by the body, so you don't have to be overly zealous, but you should not let much in. Besides, too many woody stems will taint the wine.

When foraging for elderberries gather clusters that have all ripened, because you don't want any bitter green berries on the stem. Even having some berries dried like tiny raisins can be preferable.

continued

INGREDIENTS

4 pounds (2 kg) elderberries

3 pounds (1.5 kg) sugar

1 gallon plus 1½ cups (5 L) boiling filtered or unchlorinated water

Juice of 1 lemon or 1 teaspoon citric acid or 1 teaspoon acid blend (depending on preference and availability)

1 teaspoon pectic enzyme

1 teaspoon yeast nutrient

Yeast recommendations: one 5-gram packet of Gervin GV2–Robust wine yeast or Vintner's Harvest wine yeast–VR21 or R56

INSTRUCTIONS

1. Clean and sterilize your fermentation bin and carboy, as well as a masher (if using).

2. Take the berries off their stalks and place in the fermentation bin. I use a plastic fork for this job.

3. Squeeze out as much juice as you can using a masher; do this firmly but gently, squishing them in but trying not to crush the seeds inside. You could also use your hands, but be prepared to use a lot of soap to get them back to their original color.

4. Add the sugar and pour over 2 pints (1 L) of the boiling water. Stir until the sugar has fully dissolved. Add the rest of the water and the lemon and yeast nutrient. Take a hydrometer reading if you wish to know how strong it is.

5. Check that the temperature is below 90°F (32°C) and then add the yeast and pectic enzyme. Ideally, this should be made into a yeast starter, but if that sounds too technical, sprinkling a packet over the must (unfermented wine) still works. Some will add sulphites at this stage. I've never felt the need, but it's a personal choice: sulphites will give an extra level of security against spoilage and therefore the novice brewer may want to use them in order to learn how to brew without complications before they are willing to take the risk.

6. Leave to stand for three to four days so the vigorous fermentation can happen.

7. Siphon into your carboy or demijohn and then leave for around a month.

8. After a month, siphon into another demijohn, leaving the lees (a.k.a. sediment) behind. This process is called racking and should be repeated between one and three more times depending on how much sediment builds up. I top up with boiled then cooled water each time as you will lose some liquid. Take a hydrometer reading after each racking and at room temperature. As soon as the reading is stable for three days your wine is ready to bottle. Cold temperatures may pause the fermentation process, so if you are not sure then move your demijohn to somewhere warmer. The steadier the temperature is kept during the secondary fermentation the better.

9. When ready, siphon your wine into sterilized bottles adding corks. Don't be tempted to use screw tops unless you want your wine to taste like a really bad sherry. Let your wine sit for at least a month, if not a year or two, before drinking. If worried that this is an impossibility in your house, make 10 times this amount and hide as much as you can!

Note: *You can freeze the berries overnight on their stems, as this makes it easier to pry them loose off the stems. It also breaks the skin and allows juice to run more freely when squeezing.*

Not-So-Alcoholic Wild Yeast Elderflower "Champagne"

YIELD: 2 gallons (8 L) "champagne"   SUGGESTED FERMENTATION VESSEL: 2-gallon (8-L) fermentation bin
PREP TIME: 4 hours   MINIMUM FERMENTATION TIME: 4 days and an additional 3 weeks

This recipe is entitled "not-so-alcoholic" because it does contain a little alcohol, enough to concern those who can't drink for religious or health reasons.That said, the alcohol content is nothing like that of Alcoholic Elderflower "Champagne" (page 70)!

This alcohol-light concoction is a refreshing reminder of lazy summer days, and the delicately perfumed scent of elderflower is a delight to drink.

This recipe relies on wild yeast, something that might be hard to come by in some areas. I have certainly heard that those living high up in apartment blocks in cities can struggle to find wild yeasts in the air, due to the lack of living organisms 12 stories up. If yours doesn't start fermenting after three or four days, you can always cheat a little by adding some champagne yeast.

Pick the elderflowers early on a dry and bright summer's morning as the pollen on the elderflowers is higher and it will taste better. Sometimes you get a smell akin to cat urine from elder and that is an indication that there isn't much pollen on the flowers. The more pollen the better the flavor. In order to obtain the elderflowers needed for this recipe, please refer to the recipe for Alcoholic Elderflower "Champagne" on page 70.

INGREDIENTS

6 large elderflower heads

2 gallons (8 L) filtered or unchlorinated water

2.2 pounds (1 kg) sugar

¼ cup rose petals

Juice of 4 lemons

3 tablespoons white wine vinegar (or Persimmon Vinegar, see page 86)

INSTRUCTIONS

1. While you sterilize your fermentation vessel, leave the elderflowers on some dry paper for a couple of hours to allow any insects to leave home. Meanwhile, boil the water, stir in the sugar until it is dissolved, and allow this to cool to room temperature.

2. Using a fork, remove the elderflowers from the stems and let them drop into the fermentation vessel. Add the sugar solution and the rest of the ingredients.

3. Cover with a clean tea towel or similar and leave at around 70°F (20°C) for at least four days to one week. Check periodically to ensure that there is no mold forming and that it has started to bubble.

4. You now need to strain it into bottles. At this stage the bottles can be rather volatile, so I recommend using good-quality swing-top bottles if you can get hold of them. It's ready to drink immediately and will continue to ferment for at least another week. Once fermented it should be consumed within about two weeks. I once made 200 pints of elderflower champagne and it lasted for 18 months or more, and so I can vouch that it will keep for longer than the two weeks I suggest! It is, however, at its freshest within the first two weeks.

CHAPTER 3

Condiments and Appetizers

The term *condiment* is believed to come from the Latin *condimentum*, which can be used to mean spice, seasoning, sauce, or relish. The Romans were certainly fond of their condiments.

Their favorite was garum, a kind of fish sauce that was passed on from ancient Greek culture. The Romans loved this stuff so much they would rival the Americans' addiction to yellow mustard and tomato ketchup. The best garum would sell for a price equivalent to the finest bottles of wine. Roman soldiers would march with their own supply so that they would never run out. A quick glance at some historical Roman recipes suggests that almost every dish contained some sort of garum.

Condiments are well known for improving the flavor of bland foods and in aiding digestion. It's impossible to really know for certain who first started using them, though I suspect whoever it was picked many plants and used them as a crude accompaniment to foraged or cooked food. Indeed,

some research suggests that plants like chilies and mustards might actually have been cultivated generations before wheat and other cereal grains.

What is certain is that all cultures use condiments to enhance their dishes and, in some cases, for medicinal purposes. In India, an ancient and still widely used remedy for people suffering a lack of appetite is a few mustard seeds in warm milk taken before their meal, as mustard improves saliva production. Saliva both moistens our food so it can be swallowed more easily and contains an enzyme called amylase, which helps break down starches into sugars. In other words, mustard can kick-start your digestion before your food even reaches your stomach. This is perhaps why mustard is the most widely used condiment (by volume) in the world.

Fermented Ketchup

YIELD: 1 pint (500 ml) ketchup   SUGGESTED JAR SIZE: 1 pint (500 ml)
PREP TIME: 5 minutes   FERMENTATION TIME: 3 to 5 days

If you are like 97 percent of American households, then you are sure to have a bottle of tomato ketchup knocking around in your kitchen. Nothing could be more American, right? Well no, not according to Jasmine Wiggins, writing in *National Geographic*.

It's an odd-sounding word when you think of it, tomato ketchup, and this is because it's not English. It comes from *kê-tsiap*, a Hokkien Chinese word, and is a sauce with the same name made using fermented fish. From these origins it slowly developed first in the United Kingdom, where tomatoes were added, and then in the United States where a half-German gentleman named Heinz decided it needed more sugar and vinegar in order keep the contents preserved.

This recipe rewinds tomato ketchup to a

time before vinegar was used to halt fermentation and when fish sauce was an essential part of it. However, if you are vegetarian, vegan, or simply don't like fish, then you can omit fish sauce from the recipe. In fact the same could be said about all the spices too, as these can be chopped and changed to your liking. Because my son, Loki, is the biggest consumer of tomato ketchup in our house, I added his favorite spice, cinnamon. He loves this version of tomato ketchup. In fact the first time I placed some in front of him he demolished half the jar.

INGREDIENTS

2½ cups (330 g) tomato paste (see the following recipe to make your own)

½ cup raw honey or maple syrup

¼ cup liquid from a previous ferment

¼ cup fish sauce (optional)

1 tablespoon sea salt

½ teaspoon celery salt

½ teaspoon cinnamon

¼ teaspoon ground allspice

INSTRUCTIONS

1. Add all the ingredients to a mixing bowl and thoroughly combine.

2. Pour into a mason jar. If you don't have a spout on your mixing bowl, then a jam funnel may come in handy at this point, as it can be a sloppy business otherwise. Alternatively, you could just mix in a jug.

   Those using store-bought tomato paste (or who have dramatically reduced their own paste) may find at this point that the sauce is a little too thick. If this is the case, just stir in some filtered or unchlorinated water until the sauce reaches your desired consistency. Depending on how much you add, you may need to use an extra jar.

3. Loosely cover your jar(s) with a small piece of material or airlock and leave to ferment on the countertop for three to five days before refrigerating, ensuring that there is a tang of fermentation.

4. Consume within three to six months, although in all truth it will probably keep for much longer.

continued

How to Make Tomato Paste for Tomato Ketchup

YIELD: 1 pint (500 ml) tomato paste

SUGGESTED JAR SIZE: 1 pint (500 ml)

PREP TIME: 1 minute, and 10 minutes stirring time

By making your own paste you will ensure that it is additive free. It can also be a great way to use up any glut you may have from growing your own tomatoes. The resulting paste can be frozen and used when needed.

INGREDIENTS

5 pounds (2.2 kg) tomatoes

½ to 1 cup extra virgin olive oil

1 teaspoon sea salt

INSTRUCTIONS

1. Using only ripe tomatoes, roughly chop and remove the stems. Also check the tomatoes for any damage or bruising; discard any offending fruit.

2. Place the chopped tomatoes into a large saucepan.

3. Bring the tomatoes to a boil and keep on a high heat for two to three minutes until they start to soften a little. Be careful not to overboil or stand too close, as tomatoes seem to turn to hot lava when they are cooking.

4. Pour in ½ cup of the olive oil and the sea salt. This whole process makes the tomatoes much easier to manage. Use more of the olive oil as required.

5. In order to remove the seeds and pulp, push the tomatoes through a sieve.

6. This stage is to reduce the tomatoes down, and it takes a lot of time; don't worry though as you don't have to be hands-on for much of the process. You can use one of two methods to simmer the sauce: If using a roasting pan, put into an oven on medium-low heat, 300°F (150°C), stirring every 20 to 30 minutes for the next three hours. After this time reduce the heat to low heat at 250°F (120°C) and repeat the process for another two hours until the tomato pulp is thick and dark. If using a pot to simmer, put the sauce on a low heat for 30 to 90 minutes, until it has reduced by at least half. The latter will need more stirring to ensure you don't end up with tomato caramel stuck to the bottom of your pan—about once every 10 minutes will do the job. Keep this up until the pulp has become thick and darkened in color. A good indicator is to keep an eye on the color of the splats of tomato on the side of the saucepan; if they are starting to turn very dark, you are not stirring enough. I cannot emphasize enough in the process about how important it is to keep checking, as leaving pulp for too long

will result in scorching. You can of course take a break and do this in shifts if you need to get on with your life—simply remove your tomatoes from the heat source and return them when you come back to it.

7. If all of this seems far too much effort, then fear not and instead whip up a tin of tomatoes in a food processor, and then boil gently for approximately 40 minutes, stirring frequently.

8. Whichever method you choose, allow it to cool before making your tomato ketchup (see Fermented Ketchup on page 80).

Fermented Horseradish Sauce

YIELD: 1 cup horseradish sauce   SUGGESTED JAR SIZE: ½ pint (250 ml)
PREP TIME: 20 minutes   FERMENTATION TIME: 5 days

I wrote this recipe with tears streaming down my cheeks. Just making it seemed to help clear up a cold that was threatening to send me to bed! This is a great recipe for the winter months, and it goes well with meats, traditionally roast beef.

INGREDIENTS

1 cup horseradish root (one skinny root or half a fat one)

¼ cup liquid from a previous ferment (if available)

1 teaspoon honey

¼ cup (60 ml) filtered or unchlorinated water, plus a little more if needed

1 teaspoon sea salt

INSTRUCTIONS

1. Rinse and peel the root, then grate it. It does give off some fumes, so you might want to wear goggles. (I don't, but that's just me. You have to be the judge of your own tolerance levels.)

2. Add the root to your food processor and blend slowly, pouring in the liquid from a previous ferment (if using), the honey, and, if need be, a little water. You are looking for the consistency of hummus. If your root is looking a little dry, you can add more water.

3. Scoop the pulp into a half pint (250 ml) jar and loosely put the lid over it. Make up a brine with the ¼ cup water and the salt, allow to cool, and then pour over the top of the sauce. Some of this will absorb into the sauce, but really it is a barrier for any mold taking hold, so try not to mix it into the sauce.

4. Loosely put some material over the top of your jar. Leave to ferment for at least five days, although if left for a little longer, it can mellow out a little more. Start tasting after three days—let your taste be the judge of when it is ready.

5. This will keep in the refrigerator for up to about six months.

Cultured Mustard

YIELD: ¼ cup (2 oz; 60 ml) mustard   SUGGESTED JAR SIZES: ½ pint (250 ml) for fermenting; then decant into smaller 2-ounce (50 ml) jars
PREP TIME: 10 minutes   FERMENTATION TIME: 3 to 4 days

This very simple recipe creates a more tangy mustard than you may be used to, and adds another dimension to a time-honored American favorite. It's made using seeds. I did experiment with using mustard powder, but I found that once drained the return was miserly.

INGREDIENTS

1 cup (240 ml) filtered or unchlorinated water

¾ cup raw apple cider vinegar

4 ounces (120 g) yellow mustard seeds

4 ounces (120 g) bold black mustard seeds

1 tablespoon sea salt

INSTRUCTIONS

1. Place all the ingredients into a ½-pint (250 ml) jar and stir well. I like to use a wooden chopstick for stirring ferments such as this one, as it helps to pinpoint the rogue mustard seeds that stick to the side of the jar. Although I like to steer clear of plastic at any given opportunity, I would also recommend placing a water-filled zip-top bag over the top of this ferment. As, try as you might, there will always be a few mustard seeds above the water-line. If you have an airlock, then using that will certainly have the same effect.

2. Cover with a small piece of fabric, and then leave the jar in a cool, dark spot for three to four days.

3. Once fermented you can transfer into smaller jars and give away as presents. Remember to keep refrigerated and use within a year or so.

Persimmon Vinegar

YIELD: 1 cup (8 oz; 250 ml) vinegar   SUGGESTED JAR SIZE: 1 quart (1 L)
PREP TIME: 30 minutes (over a period of days)   FERMENTATION TIME: 1 week

Persimmon vinegar can be used as a drinking vinegar, much like the shrub, a classic American beverage that features vinegared syrup. The original recipe for Korean persimmon vinegar is to simply put all your persimmons into a tub and leave them for a few months. This recipe, by contrast, uses raw apple cider vinegar to get it started and takes a lot less time. It is based on what I could translate from various Korean sources.

INGREDIENTS

1½ pounds (700 g) persimmons
¼ cup raw apple cider vinegar

INSTRUCTIONS

Day 1 to 3

1. Cut the stem off the fruit, and then cut most of them in half and a few into quarters. Sterilize a quart-size jar and then add the fruit halves and quarters one by one; the quarters help to plug the gaps. Add a weight to the top, then cover the jar with a small piece of material and a rubber band, and leave it at room temperature in a dark spot for three to four days.

Day 4 to 18

1. Check that the fruit has started to ferment and also to ensure there is no mold forming. I'm afraid you'll have to start again if there is any mold. Always ensure you have checked the top fruits, as sometimes the fermentation process can push them up and over the jar.

    The liquid in the jar should have risen, and it will now be covering the fruits. If not, then push them down a little. I sneak a taste at this point and it should start to taste fruity, tart, and delicious. Ensuring you have reapplied the weight in the jar and the material over it, return your jar to its dark place for an additional two weeks.

If at some point during this time you look at your jar and see a white layer has formed over and around the persimmons, a layer that resembles some kind of glue, don't worry as this is the new mother forming. At this point, you can jump to the directions for day 18, as in my experience this layer will spread and grow harder and harder until it is difficult to get any vinegar from your persimmons. (See the discussion in the Author's Note on page 6 about "mothers.")

Day 18

1. Strain the fruit by lining a sterilized sieve or colander with cheesecloth and setting it over a sterilized bowl—to be double cautious about rogue microbes you can iron the cheesecloth too as this will further sterilize it. Then pour the liquid from the jar through the cheesecloth; you'll also need to scoop out the now very mushy persimmons on the cheesecloth and then fold over the edges and put a plate or lid over it to keep flies at bay. This ensures that all the liquid escapes. Be patient and don't squeeze, as it can add a haze to your final product. This bit can take time so leave it for at least an hour.

   Once all the liquid has been strained, pour it back into your jar—check again for mold, as any signs of it mean you'll have to restart the whole process.

   At this stage you can bottle and start drinking your persimmon vinegar. I think it is delicious

at this stage; however, you may want to add a bit more time for it to condition, in which case read on.

Day 18 to 32

1. Return the material and rubber band to the top of your jar and leave in a dark place at room temperature for an additional two weeks. The vinegar will most certainly have a white layer of bacteria sitting on top of it by now. As I mentioned before, this is where it is forming a new mother. You can strain this out and reuse it for making more vinegar or compost it.

   Strain the vinegar into a bottle and drink or use as a salad dressing.

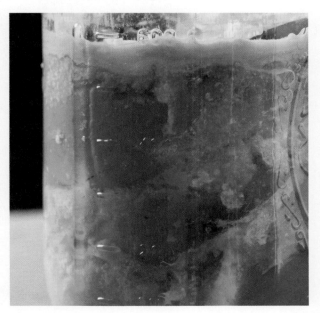

Pico de Gallo

YIELD: 1½ quarts (1½ L) pico de gallo   SUGGESTED JAR SIZES: 1 quart (1 L) and 1 pint (500 ml)
PREP TIME: 20 to 40 minutes   FERMENTATION TIME: 3 to 5 days

Whenever we throw a party, one of the first things to be made is fresh pico de gallo. It's similar to salsa but with less liquid. It can be scooped up with tortilla chips for a fresh burst of flavor. This fermented version uses more liquid because the fresh ingredients are submerged in brine. This creates a sour twist on the popular favorite.

This recipe is adapted from one I found in *Real Food Fermentation* by Alex Lewin. He recommends trying it with grilled fish and chicken. He also recommends peeling and coring the tomatoes if you don't want the extra flavor from the skins. I tend to leave them on as the nutritional value of this condiment is drastically increased by doing so.

INGREDIENTS

6 tomatoes (1 lb 4 oz; 600 g)

6 garlic cloves

1 onion

2 chili peppers

1 small bunch cilantro (4 oz; 100 g)

2 cups (500 ml) filtered or unchlorinated cold water

1 tablespoon sea salt

Pepper

2 tablespoons liquid from a previous ferment (if available)

INSTRUCTIONS

1. If you want to use skinned tomatoes, score an X in the base of each tomato and plunge them into boiling water—use tongs or a slotted spoon, then plunge them into cold water. This makes it easier to peel them.

2. Chop the tomatoes into small pieces and place them into a large mixing bowl.

3. Press the garlic cloves under the thick edge of the knife to crush them, which makes it easier to take off the peel, then either put through a garlic crusher or mincer, or slice them into tiny pieces. Place into the mixing bowl.

4. Cut the onion and chilies into small pieces and chuck them in too.

5. Chop up the cilantro and throw that in, then massage the whole lot with your hands. You can stop at this point if you just want to use fresh pico de gallo. Continue if you want to ferment it.

6. Make up the brine by boiling enough water to dissolve the sea salt, then stir it together before topping up with the remaining cold water. I find ½ to 1 cup of boiled water is enough.

7. Add some pepper to taste, then transfer the whole lot to a 2-quart (2-L) jar. I find there is a bit of headspace at the top. Push down on the pico de gallo, pour over the liquid from a previous ferment if you can, then top up with the brine. You will need to keep the contents submerged. Cover with a piece of material or an airlock if using.

8. Place in a warm spot out of direct sunlight and leave for three to five days until it has reached your preferred level of fermentation.

9. Once ready, throw a party and use it all up. Alternatively, you can keep it in the refrigerator and use within a month. It starts to lose some of its color after that time, though it is still edible and good but just not as pleasing to the eye.

Fermented Pepper Hummus

YIELD: 2 cups (500 ml) hummus   SUGGESTED JAR SIZE: 1 quart (1 L)

PREP TIME: 20 minutes   FERMENTATION TIME: 3 days

Hummus is one of the most widely known foods from the Middle East. This twist on it creates a tangy dip that will intrigue your guests, whether they are visiting to watch the Super Bowl or just to sample the food in your super bowls!

INGREDIENTS

2 cups (500 ml) filtered or unchlorinated water

1 tablespoon sea salt

2 red bell peppers (about 10 oz; 300 g)

6 garlic cloves

For the hummus

Fermented red pepper and garlic, drained and patted dry

2 cups chickpeas, either canned or soaked overnight and drained

2 tablespoons tahini paste

1 tablespoon lemon juice

1 tablespoon olive oil

1 teaspoon paprika

Pinch of cayenne pepper (optional)

INSTRUCTIONS

1. Heat the water and stir in the salt until dissolved. Put to one side to cool.

2. Meanwhile, cut out the white bits from the peppers and knock out the seeds. Then cut into rings and pack lightly into a quart-size jar. Pop in a clove of peeled garlic and every now and then pour over the brine, ensuring the peppers are fully submerged.

3. Leave to ferment for three days.

For the hummus

1. Drain the peppers and garlic and pat until very dry. You can also place them into a square of muslin cloth, and apply pressure to squeeze out more moisture.

2. Put the chickpeas and tahini in a food processor and mix until it makes a paste. Add the lemon juice, olive oil, and spices.

3. Next, add the peppers slowly and continue mixing in the food processor; you may not need to use all of them. As the peppers retain a fair amount of moisture, they can water down the hummus. Keep adding until you are happy with the consistency.

Don't worry if it is a little too watery still, you can always strain it again through some muslin cloth until it reaches the desired consistency.

4. Keep refrigerated and use within three weeks.

Easy Apple Cider Vinegar

YIELD: 1 pint (500 ml) vinegar   SUGGESTED JAR SIZE: 1 widemouthed quart (1 L)
PREP TIME: 3 minutes   FERMENTATION TIME: 2 to 3 weeks

The process of making vinegar is as old as time itself. After so many years of trying to stop my wine from turning into vinegar it seems odd to now be trying to make vinegar. Making this vinegar is similar to making Persimmon Vinegar (page 86), although due to the water content here you get a higher volume of vinegar.

This recipe is a great way to use up fallen or bruised fruit or even any scraps of apples (cores and peelings) left over from making apple dishes. I'd suggest using only wild or organic apples to make this vinegar, because a high amount of pesticides are used on store-bought, nonorganic apples. If the price of organic apples makes you balk a little, then hunt through your neighborhood in the fall. Chances are you'll find at least one crab apple tree desperate to have its fruit used!

Sometimes the cider vinegar will develop a mother (see image), especially when left for a while. Far from being a problem this is a great asset, as it can be used to create more vinegar. Simply pop the mother in some apple cider and it will get to work turning it into another batch of vinegar. (See the discussion in the Author's Note on page 6 about "mothers.")

INGREDIENTS

4 to 6 small to medium apples*

2 cups (500 ml) filtered or unchlorinated water

5 teaspoons sugar

* A small apple will weigh approximately 3½ ounces (100 g)

INSTRUCTIONS

1. Roughly cut up the apples and toss them—stalks, pips, and all—into a widemouthed 1-quart jar.

2. Boil 1 cup of the water and stir in the sugar until fully dissolved.

3. Add the sugar solution to the rest of the water and pour over the apples. Ensure there is a bit of breathing room at the top.

4. Affix a small piece of material over the top and secure with a rubber band or use an airlock.

5. Leave the jar in a dark place for two to three weeks, stirring with a wooden spoon every few days. Give it a taste after this time; if it tastes like a sweeter version of the vinegar you are used to, then it is done.

6. Once it *is* done, strain into sterilized bottles. I store mine in a dark cupboard along with my other vinegars and use within a few months. Some people choose to keep theirs in the refrigerator.

Easy Plum Vinegar

YIELD: 1 pint (500 ml) vinegar   SUGGESTED JAR SIZE: 1 widemouthed quart (1 L)
PREP TIME: 30 minutes   FERMENTATION TIME: 2 to 3 weeks

The recipe for Easy Apple Cider Vinegar on page 92 can be adapted for any fruit, such as plums. Whenever I go picking from a plum tree there seem to be more plums on the ground than on the tree, so I thought it would make sense to make a plum vinegar. You'll notice the prep time is considerably longer than the apple version. This is to account for the occasional plum that refuses to come loose from its stone.

Plum vinegar is sweeter than many other vinegars, making it a great salad dressing.

INGREDIENTS

About 15 to 20 plums

3 cups (750 ml) filtered or unchlorinated water (approximately)

5 teaspoons sugar

INSTRUCTIONS

1. Chop the plums in half, ensuring that you cut out the hard stone from the middle of the fruit and retain as much of the pulp as possible. Then place the plum pieces into a widemouthed 1-quart jar.

2. Boil 1 cup of the water and stir in the sugar until fully dissolved. Add the sugar solution to the rest of the water and pour over the plums. Ensure there is a bit of breathing room at the top. Affix a small piece of material or an airlock over the top.

3. Leave the jar in a dark place for two to three weeks, stirring with a wooden spoon every few days. Don't forget to try a little at this time, although I have to say I found it quite addictive and wanted to try some every morning!

4. After two or three weeks there should be a mother forming. It will taste unmistakably vinegary. If it is still sweet, then leave for a little longer or add a tablespoon of any other raw vinegar you have.

5. Once it *is* done, strain into a sterilized bottle. I store mine in a dark cupboard along with my other vinegars and use within a few months. Some choose to keep theirs in the refrigerator.

Fermented Mayonnaise

YIELD: 8 ounces (250 ml) mayonnaise   SUGGESTED JAR SIZE: ½ pint (250 ml)
PREP TIME: 5 minutes   FERMENTATION TIME: 8 hours

The first time I made mayonnaise it was a complete disaster. I was a typical college student at the time, meaning I was short on funds, and so this was a double disaster because I used up much of the week's food budget on making something I couldn't use. I realize now that my simple mistake was to pour in the olive oil too quickly. As a result, no matter what I did, I couldn't get it to combine.

As with many homemade condiments this is much better than store-bought. I find its fermented tang pairs extremely well on top of a juicy burger. If you are vegetarian and want to eat like they do in Belgium, try some on your french fries.

INGREDIENTS

1 medium egg

1 teaspoon French-style Dijon mustard or Cultured Mustard (page 85)

¼ teaspoon sea salt

1 cup (250 ml) canola or rapeseed oil, or extra virgin olive oil if you prefer

1 tablespoon liquid from a previous ferment (if available)

1 tablespoon lemon juice

INSTRUCTIONS

1.   Mix the egg, mustard, and salt by pulsing in your food processor until it has gone a dark, uniform yellow.

2.   Next, slowly pour in the oil. If using a food processor, I find that blending using a pulsing action works well and gives you time to be mindful of how the mayo is looking. If using a hand blender, I'd suggest blending in a container that is big enough to hold just the business end of your

blender and to jig it up and down as you blend in the oil, again being very slow and keeping a keen eye on what you are doing. If you notice that the oil is sitting on top of the eggs and not blending in, then stop pouring and keep blending. You can pour again when it has started to combine.

3. Once blended to a nice consistent yellow color with a creamy consistency, pour in the liquid from a previous ferment, if using, and lemon juice and give that the tiniest of mixes.

4. Pour into a jar and secure a clean piece of material or an airlock and leave in your fermentation spot for eight hours. Your mayonnaise should have a small, foamy skin formed on the top of it. Dip your finger through it and have a taste—it should have a refreshing tang.

5. Return the lid to the jar, refrigerate, and consume within a fortnight. You will notice that this mayonnaise is waterier than you might be used to.

Fermented Aioli

YIELD: 8 ounces (250 ml) aioli   SUGGESTED JAR SIZE: ½ pint (250 ml)

PREP TIME: 5 minutes   FERMENTATION TIME: 8 hours

At a glance, aioli seems to be like mayonnaise. When eating it in France, I have even heard restaurant servers describe it as such. It is sort of true, albeit for two important ingredients: garlic and olive oil. If you have only ever tried mayonnaise before, I strongly urge you to have a go at making this condiment—especially if you have eaten only store-bought mayo in a squirt jar. I think you will be pleasantly rewarded. Do be warned though: the taste is far stronger than that of your usual mayonnaise, so be prepared for a jolt of flavor!

INGREDIENTS

3 garlic cloves*

2 egg yolks

1 teaspoon French-style Dijon mustard or Cultured Mustard (page 85)

¼ teaspoon sea salt

1 cup (250 ml) extra virgin olive oil

1 tablespoon liquid from a previous ferment (if available)

1 tablespoon lemon juice

* You can use the Brined Garlic on page 122 for more lacto goodness

INSTRUCTIONS

1. Peel the garlic; I find it is easier to peel if you smash it with the thick end of a knife or a rolling pin before peeling. Once peeled you can either mince it in your food processor or smash it up in a mortar and pestle.

2. Now mix the garlic with the egg yolks, mustard, and salt by pulsing in your food processor. You are looking for it to be a uniform yellow color.

3. Next, for the olive oil, the key in making aioli is in blending the oil correctly. Get it wrong and it will separate. If using a food processor, I find a pulsing action works well, and if using a hand blender, I'd suggest blending in a container that is big enough to hold just the business end of your blender and to jig it up and down as you blend in the oil. In both cases, pour in very slowly as your aim is to pour a thin steady stream, and remember, too, to ensure the oil doesn't just sit over the top of your eggs. If that happens, then stop pouring and keep blending until it is thoroughly combined and is that lovely dark yellow color again.

4. Once blended to the nice dark yellow color and a slightly fluffy consistency, pour in the liquid from a previous ferment, if using, and lemon juice and give it the tiniest of mixes.

5. Pour into a ½-pint (250-ml) jar and secure a clean piece of material over the top with a rubber band or affix an airlock and leave in your fermentation spot for eight hours.

6. If there is a small skin on the top, then it is ready. Return the lid to the jar, refrigerate, and consume within a fortnight. It's worth mentioning that fermented aioli is waterier than you might be used to.

Coconut Chutney

YIELD: 8 ounces (250 ml) chutney   SUGGESTED JAR SIZE: ½ pint (250 ml)
PREP TIME: 30 minutes   FERMENTATION TIME: 3 to 5 days

In South India coconut chutney is a breakfast staple, served with Rice Flour Dosas (page 182) or Rice Flour Idlis (page 179). Usually it is made fresh, but this version can be made in a batch in advance and kept in the refrigerator until needed. Because it is fermented, you get the added benefits of lactobacilli bacteria with your breakfast. Lentils contain around 13 percent of prebiotic carbohydrates, which help the good bacteria get to work. Making dosas or idlis and coconut chutney is an ideal combination for good health and great taste.

There are many variations on this recipe, with some even claiming to be "the authentic." But in the end it comes down to personal preference. There isn't really an authentic recipe for chutney, just like there isn't an "authentic" beer recipe or cider blend. If you like your chutney simple, then use just the coconut. But most agree that the chana daal adds something to the texture and depth. If you like other spices in addition to the ones I suggest here, then add them as well. Please experiment and have fun!

INGREDIENTS

3 tablespoons chana daal (rehydrated) or 3 tablespoons chickpeas

1 cup fresh or shredded coconut

2 tablespoons coconut oil, ghee, or vegetable oil for frying

1 tablespoon coconut treacle, honey, or maple syrup

2 tablespoons tamarind paste or lemon juice

1 teaspoon sea salt

½ teaspoon yellow mustard seeds

1 teaspoon ground cumin

1 teaspoon coriander seed

1 hot chili (optional), sliced

¾ cup (190 ml) Kefir (page 254) or Yogurt (page 260)

Pinch of asafoetida powder (if available)

INSTRUCTIONS

1. Soak the chana daal for at least four hours. If using dried, shredded coconut, rehydrate that too by placing it in a bowl of water.

2. Strain the chana daal. Place the coconut oil in a frying pan and cook the chana daal on medium heat for about five minutes, until it goes a little darker in color.

3. Transfer to a mixing bowl and mix the daal and the coconut, along with the coconut treacle, tamarind paste, and salt.

4. It's optional but at this stage you can also gently fry up the mustard seeds, cumin, and coriander seeds in another frying pan until they are just browned, as this will help bring out their flavor. (You may even wish to add the hot chili if you like a little kick in your coconut chutney—although some would say this is sacrilegious!). Some choose to add these ingredients without frying or just frying the mustard seeds; again it is your preference that dictates, although I would strongly recommend at least frying the mustard seeds.

5. Add the spices, half of the kefir, and the asafoetida powder to the frying pan to combine all the flavors and let this reach a sizzle. Then remove from the heat. (If you can't find asafoetida powder or if you want to omit it if you are gluten intolerant, don't worry; it is not essential.) Stir in the rest of the kefir, then blend together with the coconut and daal.

6. You can eat the chutney fresh at this point or transfer it to an 8-ounce jar. To ferment, place in your usual fermentation spot out of direct sunlight and cover with a piece of material or an airlock to keep out the flies. Pick up the jar after two days and check for air bubbles; if there are none, then leave for an additional two days, then refrigerate. Use within six weeks.

Note: *To unshell a coconut, forcibly tap it with the back of a knife. Turn the coconut with each hit. The wooden part should shatter, leaving an egg-like center that can be peeled like a potato.*

Hot Chili Sauce

YIELD: 7 ounces (200 g) chili sauce   SUGGESTED JAR SIZE: 8 ounces (250 ml) if available, 1 pint (500 ml) if not
PREP TIME: 5 to 10 minutes   FERMENTATION TIME: 2 to 4 days

One of the most ubiquitous sauces, after mustard and mayo, has to be hot chili sauce. I have heard it argued that chilies were the first foodstuff ever to be cultivated, making this possibly the oldest recipe in this book.

Chili sauce can be served with a variety of dishes to give them an extra bit of kick. My personal favorite use is to add it to Cheddar cheese and spinach for the filling of a dosa. I also use it in my cooking arsenal to help add flavor to stocks, stews, and of course, chili con carne.

INGREDIENTS
½ cup (125 ml) filtered or unchlorinated cold water
1 teaspoon sea salt
8 to 10 chilies

INSTRUCTIONS

1. Make up the brine by boiling some of the water and then stirring in the salt. I found 2 tablespoons of boiling water enough to dissolve 1 teaspoon of sea salt. Top up with the rest of the cold water.

2. Take the green stems off the top of the chilies. The next step is a matter of choice: You can cut the chilies in half and then either scrape out the pith and seeds for a milder chili sauce or you can leave them in for a hotter sauce.

3. Next, cut the chilies into small rounds, or semicircles if you have cut them in half.

4. Pop the chilies into your jar and then top up with the brine.

5. Put a weight or water-filled zip-top bag on the chilies so they sit below the waterline; they can be rather buoyant! Cover and leave in your usual fermentation spot out of direct sunlight to ferment.

6. After two to four days, strain off the brine and blitz the chilies in a food processor. You can add some of the brine back in for a more liquid sauce. Refrigerate and use within six months.

Note: *Contrary to popular belief, the seeds do not contain capsicum, the chemical that makes chilies hot. This is actually located in the white pith on the inside of the chili, which is why when you scrape them, they are not as hot as unscraped.*

Sriracha Sauce

YIELD: ½ pint (250 ml) sriracha sauce   SUGGESTED JAR SIZE: ½ pint (250 ml)
PREP TIME: 20 minutes   FERMENTATION TIME: 5 to 10 days

Thailand is firmly on the backpackers' trail, and those intrepid explorers who have explored its delights have returned back with tales of a hot sauce that rivals any other.

INGREDIENTS

2 cups (500 ml) filtered or unchlorinated water

1 teaspoon sea salt

10 to 20 hot chilies

4 garlic cloves (approximately 1 oz; 30 g)

2 ounces (60 g) jaggery (if available), or brown sugar

1 tablespoon fish sauce

2 tablespoons rice vinegar (optional)

INSTRUCTIONS

1. Make the brine by boiling at least 2 tablespoons of the water and then stirring in the salt until dissolved. Top up with the rest of the water.

2. Take the green stems off the top of the chilies. The next step is a matter of choice: You can cut your chilies in half and then either scrape out the piths and seeds for a milder chili sauce or you can leave the pith in for a hotter sauce.

3. Next, cut the chilies into small rounds—or semicircles if you have cut them in half.

4. Pop the chilies into your jar along with the garlic and top up with the brine. Leave to ferment for 5 to 10 days or longer, depending on taste.

5. Strain the chilies and keep the brine.

6. Add the jaggery and fish sauce to your food processor and blend until it has made a course paste. Keep adding the brine until it reaches your desired consistency, although I wouldn't add more than ½ cup or the sauce will be very watery.

7. Taste the sauce. If you like it to have a bit more body, then you can add the rice vinegar. Add ¼ teaspoon at a time, mix very well, and keep tasting until it is perfect. Keep refrigerated and use within six months.

Kombucha

YIELD: 5 gallons (19 L) kombucha   SUGGESTED FERMENTATION VESSEL: 5 gallon (19 L)
PREP TIME: 2 hours   FERMENTATION TIME: 1 week

Kombucha is drunk frequently in some communities, and it's used as a panacea. It is suggested that daily ingestion will cure everything from the flu to cancer. I can find studies and reviews that both back this up and completely dispute it, so you'll have to make up your own mind about its medicinal qualities.

Kombucha is very easy to make. I have found that, unlike beer brewing, the fermentation process of kombucha requires very little effort by the brewer to get it right.

As a beer brewer I am used to making larger batches, and this recipe for kombucha will brew 5 gallons. If, however, you do not want to brew quite that amount, then just flip over to the recipe for Small-Batch Kombucha on page 107.

INGREDIENTS

1 pound (500 g) black tea leaves
5 gallons (19 L) filtered or unchlorinated water
1 pound (500 g) sugar
1 scoby starter culture

INSTRUCTIONS

1. Put the tea leaves into a cheesecloth and tie a knot in it so that the tea stays inside and you have one massive tea bag. Essentially, you are making a massive cup of tea that you will then ferment! Bring 1 gallon of the water to a boil and stir in the sugar. When fully dissolved, take off the heat.

2. In a large pan, add the sugared water and the rest of the water and bring to a boil. Take off the heat, add the massive tea bag, and leave to steep for about 20 minutes. When the tea has cooled sufficiently enough to handle without scalding myself, I squeeze out as much of the tea as possible from the massive tea bag by pushing it with the back of a wooden spoon.

continued

3. Strain the liquid into your fermentation vessel; this can be anything that will hold this much liquid and won't react to the culture: food-grade plastic, stainless steel, or glass or ceramic vessels will all make first-rate fermentation vessels. See page 23 for more details about equipment.

4. Allow the tea to cool to room temperature (70 to 80°F; 21 to 26°C), and then add the starter culture. Cover loosely with a tea towel to prevent flies from entering your vessel.

5. After a week check the culture. If you see a blue or red mold, then I'm afraid something has gotten in and you will have to start again.

    If you have a pH meter and want to use it, then check that the level is around 2.5 to 3.5. But I find the best check is to drink some, and if it's not sweet anymore and a little tart, then it is ready to bottle.

6. Next, take out the scoby: Wash your hands in vinegar and pull out the scoby from the kombucha—don't forget that soap kills bacteria and that is why you can't use soapy hands.

    You may have a "mother" and a "baby" or they may be stuck together. Confused? Put simply, the baby is the somewhat affectionate term for a second mother growing on the first. You can pull them apart and either use straightaway for your next batch or put them up in a scoby hotel (see page 111).

7. You can bottle the kombucha neat and it will be flat and tart, but I think very drinkable. To bottle, use a siphon directly into a jug, then pour into clean bottles, seal, and refrigerate. Remember to keep back 1 or 2 cups of your starter culture in order to start your next batch. See page 109 for how to bottle.

8. If you find bottling too much of a chore, you can siphon into a fermentation vessel with a small faucet on it and just help yourself whenever you fancy some kombucha. That said, do be aware that it will keep on fermenting and changing. Fine if you want to explore the different flavors over the next two to three weeks, but not if you want to keep the same taste. I'd urge you to try this route at least once as it is most interesting.

Small-Batch Kombucha

YIELD: 2 quarts (2 L) kombucha   SUGGESTED JAR SIZE: 2 quarts (2 L)
PREP TIME: 2 hours   FERMENTATION TIME: 1 week

If you live in a small apartment or just don't have the space for a 5-gallon fermentation vessel, then you might want to brew a more manageable-sized batch of this delicious drink. This is the same recipe as the large-batch Kombucha (page 105), but the quantities here have been perfectly adjusted to make just 2 quarts (2 L) of this fine beverage.

Also, Small-Batch Kombucha is a great option when you can't get a hold of loose leaf tea. Making a smaller batch of kombucha with tea bags is comparatively easier and less expensive than a larger batch.

INGREDIENTS

2 quarts (2 L) filtered or unchlorinated water (approximately)

½ cup sugar

2 or 3 black tea bags or 2 to 3 teaspoons black tea (see Note)

1 scoby

1 cup (250 ml) starter liquid

INSTRUCTIONS

1. Bring the water to a boil and stir in the sugar. Then take off the heat.

2. Add the tea and leave to steep for around 20 minutes. After a short while the tea will start to cool and you can gently squeeze the tea bags or the tea in cheesecloth to get more out. Don't be too hard on the tea bags as they can easily split.

3. Now strain the liquid into your fermenting vessel; this can be anything that will hold the liquid and won't react to the culture: food-grade plastic,

continued

stainless steel, or glass or ceramic vessels all make first-rate fermentation vessels. See page 23 for more details about fermentation vessels.

4. Check that your tea has cooled to room temperature (70 to 80°F; 21 to 26°C) before adding the scoby and starter liquid. Cover loosely with a tea towel to prevent flies from entering your vessel.

5. After a week check your culture. If you see mold, then I'm afraid something has gotten in and you need to throw the whole thing out. If you have a pH meter and want to use it, then check that the level is around 2.5 to 3.5. But I find the best check is to drink some; if it's not sweet anymore and a little tart, then it is ready to bottle.

6. Wash your hands in vinegar and pull out the scoby from the kombucha. You may have a "mother" and a "baby" or they may be stuck together. You can pull them apart and either use straightaway for your next batch or put them up in a scoby hotel, which is a clean jar with enough cold tea to cover the scobies.

7. See page 109 for instructions on bottling and adding flavor to your kombucha.

Note: *When making small batches it makes sense to use tea bags. You can make your own. Simply put loose tea into a small square of cheesecloth and carefully tie up the corners to form a bag. I use a small length of string to do this.*

BOTTLING KOMBUCHA

Note that you can add some flavor and a little fizz to your kombucha. Doing so will make it more like the ones you can buy in stores.

I tend to opt for 22-ounce (750-ml) bottles, because a large bottle can be shared with food as you would a bottle of wine. It is also an excellent sized bottle for a gift; plus, the whole laborious job of bottling is made much easier when there are fewer bottles! I also go for flip-top bottles, as they are designed to flip open if the buildup of gas inside is too great, reducing (but not eliminating) the chance of accidental explosions. Be sure to use thick glass bottles with strong metal casings around the caps. There are plenty of cheaper imitations out there, but in this author's opinion, they are not fit for this purpose.

INGREDIENTS FOR FLAVORING THE LARGE BATCH OF KOMBUCHA (5 GALLONS; 19 L)

¼ cup (100 g) sugar or honey, or 4 to 5 pints (2.5 L) fruit juice

1 teaspoon herbs and/or spices per bottle (optional)

INGREDIENTS FOR FLAVORING THE SMALL BATCH

3 teaspoons (10 g) sugar or honey, or 2 cups (500 ml) fruit juice

1 teaspoon herbs and/or spices per bottle

INSTRUCTIONS

1. Follow the instructions on page 107 for brewing your Small-Batch Kombucha or page 105 for your large-batch Kombucha. After removing the scoby give your kombucha a stir.

2. In order to have the fizz, you need to kick-start the fermentation with a bit of sugar. To do that you need some actual sugar or something with sugar in it, like fruit or fruit juice. If using fruit juice, dump that straight into your bucket. You can add puréed fresh fruit at a rate of 10 percent per volume of your final brew amount. This is 4 to 5 pints per 5-gallon batch. If you are using sugar or honey, it is better to boil a little of the kombucha with the sugar in it, stirring constantly until it has fully dissolved. You can then dump this back into the fermentation vessel. Any fruit or fruit juice that you add will add flavor to your final product.

3. If you wish to add herbs or spices, they can be added at this point too. I recommend around 1 teaspoon per 16-ounce (750-ml) bottle. If using fresh herbs, you can juice them up in a juicer and then dump them in at a rate of 2 ounces (50 g) per bottle.

4. Pour the kombucha into bottles, then seal the lid of your fermentation vessel tightly.

continued

5. Leave for around four days. Some fruits with high sugar content can be quite volatile so be careful, especially in hotter states and in the summer, as bottles can be rather unstable. If after four days there is no sign of carbonation, allow two more days.

6. Refrigerate when ready. You can filter out any solids or sediment. Some choose to drink the baby scobies that can grow; they won't do a healthy individual any harm and so it is a matter of taste. Use within 60 days.

SCOBY HOTEL

Scoby is an acronym for symbiotic culture of bacteria and yeast. You need a scoby to start your kombucha. And yours might come from a local scoby hotel.

A scoby hotel is the place where you store your scobies. The hotel itself is simply a jar that's kept in a cool and calm location. It is not recommended that you refrigerate your scoby for too long, as this can damage it. It's worth noting that a scoby needs time to *come alive* when it comes out of the refrigerator, which can take up to a day.

To make your hotel you will need some sweet tea, a clean glass storage vessel the size and shape of your scoby mother, and 2 quarts (2 L) kombucha starter liquid. Ideally, this needs to have a pH of 2.5. If you don't have the apparatus to measure pH, you can simply use your good judgment.

1. Make the sweet tea using 2 quarts (2 L) boiled water, ½ cup sugar, and four tea bags. Let it cool to room temperature.
2. Mix together the starter culture and tea and pour them into a glass container.
3. Loosely cover your hotel and you are now ready to start taking guests.

SOME TIPS FOR GOOD HOUSEKEEPING

Keep your hotel somewhere cool (approximately 52°F; 11°C) and out of direct sunlight, in the dark even. Keep it in a pet-free, smoke-free environment.

Don't forget to feed your guests by adding 2 cups of sugar every six weeks along with enough liquid sweet tea to keep the scobies moist. They can keep growing and will eventually take over their container if you don't top up with enough tea.

Over time and successive brews you may find your scoby hotel getting overcrowded. I have heard of people turning theirs into a sort of vegan leather and making anything from bongo drums to slippers. I cannot vouch for this practice. Regardless, people are always on the search for scobies, so you may even choose to start selling yours.

CHAPTER 4

Vegetables

If you grow your own vegetables, I have no doubt that you've experienced at least one glut. Even if you don't grow your own, your local store may occasionally have an unbeatable offer on tomatoes, cabbages, or even garlic. It's a real shame to let all that food go to waste. But when you start fermenting everything, nothing really has to go to waste again!

There is something that feels like magic when you ferment vegetables, something transformative. It's not just that fermenting helps to lock in nutrients by making minerals more bioavailable or that it helps to make food that is already good for you much better for you, it's that it also delivers an amazing taste.

Just yesterday I tucked into a pickled cucumber. I disappeared into myself for a moment at the dinner table. I was having a moment of sheer bliss. I thought about the small pickles that I used to pick off hamburgers and realized that what I was eating was such a world away from those mass-produced, vinegar-laden, shriveled things that were my introduction to pickles. This was something else, something that I instinctively knew had the power to do me good.

It is true that most vegetables will ferment (although I wouldn't try fermenting raw potatoes), and they will all taste like a different version of what you are used to. Different combinations bring out different flavors, and each one has the power to add a moment of sheer bliss to your dinner table.

THE TANG OF KIMCHI

Just like beer, vinegar, or kojii, kimchi could do with an entire book on the subject in order to really understand it. That said, this book is called *Fermenting Everything*, not *Kimchi Everything*! Instead I offer a few paragraphs to help you better understand this much revered food.

To understand kimchi is to understand Korean culture, as Korea is kimchi's birthplace and spiritual home. It is said that kimchi runs through the veins of every Korean, and that in both North and South Korea it is not just a food but a national obsession. To make it is to know every ingredient at every point of the process. It is to understand the climate of the country and the seasons. This is because kimchi is more than just a few ingredients mixed together and placed in brine. Just as good brewers understand their yeast and master vintners know their grapes, expert makers of kimchi know their bacteria. It is those millions of bacteria cells that really make kimchi, not just the ingredients.

It wasn't until I met up with a Korean chef named Wizzy, the owner of the restaurant Sky Kong Kong in Bristol, England, that I realized just what kimchi means to some Koreans. For about an hour she told me about how, although many try to re-create it, you can't just put the ingredients of kimchi together and say you've made kimchi. This dish is more than just the sum of its parts.

I think what she was trying to say is that the real flavor in kimchi comes from the microbes, that

real kimchi has to come from Korea. And I think she might be right. One of the chief principles in kimchi making is to use your hands to mix the ingredients: massaging the cabbage and working in the chili. If you watch a Korean at work making kimchi, you'll see that they are methodical, that every bit of every ingredient seems to get touched. This means that each and every kimchi made will have a different hand taste or *sson mha son mat*. In other words, because the microbial life living on my hands is different than yours, and because yours is different than someone living in Korea or even in the next state (and perhaps even the next street), we all have a different *son mat*. And that means we will all make different kimchi.

This has been backed up by science, and according to a study by scientists from Yale and Stanford, it would appear that the bacteria on your hands reflects your lifestyle, country, and cultural influences. The study compared women in the United States with women from Tanzania. The Tanzanian women had more soil-borne bacteria on their hands, presumably because they spend more time actually touching soil.

Surprisingly, the US cohort had a higher diversity of bacteria on their hands than the Tanzanian women, and yet the Tanzanians had 11 times more actual bacteria cells than the US women. However, the diversity wasn't always as good as it seemed; the US women had a far more significant amount of the family of bacteria that included MRSA, the famous superbug.

What all this means for our kimchi is yet to be understood fully by science. I guess if you don't think that your kimchi is up to scratch, then you may have to visit South Korea and make sure you shake hands with as many people as possible!

Kimchi

YIELD: 1 quart (1 L) kimchi   SUGGESTED JAR SIZE: 1 quart (1 L)
PREP TIME: 30 minutes   FERMENTATION TIME: 3 to 5 days

This is the recipe for basic kimchi. It is a recipe that can be adapted in many ways. I've had it with and without fish sauce and am a fan of both. As with all the recipes in this book you can and should tweak it to your liking. Simply take out an ingredient or two if you don't like them and add things you do really like.

INGREDIENTS

2 pounds (1 kg) cabbage (Napa cabbage if available)

1 medium onion (about 4 oz; 115 g)

¼ cup (100 g) sea salt

1 carrot (about 2 oz; 60 g)

1 daikon radish (about 8 oz; 230 g)

1 teaspoon sliced fresh ginger

6 to 7 garlic cloves

2 tablespoons fish sauce (optional)

2 tablespoons pepper flakes or 1 fresh chili, chopped

Up to 2 cups (500 ml) filtered or unchlorinated water, if needed

INSTRUCTIONS

1. Slice the cabbage lengthwise into quarters, cut out the core, and slice up the cores into small pieces. Slice the rest of the cabbage into pieces that measure 1 to 2 inches long. The idea is for them to be bite sized, and that will depend on the size of your mouth! Dice the onion.

2. Place both the cabbage and onion in a large mixing bowl and sprinkle with the salt and massage until the cabbage is no longer crisp to the touch. Place a plate over the top and leave for three to four hours.

3. Rinse the cabbage and onion under cold water and leave to one side.

4. Thinly slice the carrot and radish.

5. Add the ginger, garlic, and fish sauce (or 2 tablespoons water if you wish to omit this) in a separate bowl. Add the pepper flakes. Combine to make a paste.

6. Add the cabbage and onion back into the bowl and mix together with the paste. I have seen people

wearing gloves to do this job. I personally do not, as I think the flavor is much better if you don't. It is a matter of personal choice, but remember that you want that bacteria in.

7. Pack the kimchi into your jar. To save a mess this can be done over your bowl. Keep pressing down as you pack the kimchi in, as it will help the water level rise. Keep the vegetables below the waterline; you may need to top up with the unfiltered water if the liquid doesn't reach above the vegetables.

8. Cover with a small piece of cloth or an airlock and leave to ferment for three to five days. Refrigerate and leave for at least a week before eating.

9. Keep refrigerated and use within six months.

Pickled Parsnip Medley

YIELD: 2 quarts (2 L) pickled parsnips   SUGGESTED JAR SIZE: two 1-quart (1-L) jars
PREP TIME: 30 minutes   FERMENTATION TIME: 2 to 7 days

I personally think that parsnips fermented on their own can be rather bland, and so they need a bit of something extra. Here, the slightly sweet aniseed taste from the fennel and celeriac root gives it that something extra. Further taste "hits" are added with the ginger and garlic. The chili, and most of the other flavors, seep into the Asian pear and create something that is soothing, hot, aniseed flavored, and earthy. Finally, the crunch of the juniper berries gives a burst of fragrant, earthy flavor every time you come across one. I have to admit that when I first experimented with this recipe I was concerned that the flavors wouldn't come together. I need not have worried, as they really do! I think what helps is that there are very different textures throughout and each holds different flavors.

INGREDIENTS

1 pound (500 g) parsnips

½ pound celeriac root

1 medium carrot

1 Florence fennel bulb (about 8 oz; 200 g)

1 medium hot chili pepper (about 11oz; 25 g)

1 inch (2 to 3 cm) fresh ginger, grated

2 garlic cloves

1 tablespoon sea salt

1 Asian pear (any size)

1 tablespoon juniper berries

1 pint filtered or unchlorinated water, if needed

INSTRUCTIONS

1. Prep your fruit and vegetables: Cut the parsnips into small batons. Peel then grate the celeriac root. There can be more crevasses than the surface of the moon on a celeriac root, and as each can contain a bit of soil or dirt, I find it's best to cut these out and offer them up to the compost. Cut the carrot into thin ribbons (or grate if you are not feeling up to it).

2. Cut the fennel bulb into bite-sized chunks. Deseed and slice the chili pepper into slices.

3. Peel and grate the ginger and peel the garlic if you haven't already.

4. Add all of this prepared food into a large unbreakable bowl and massage it together. Take your meat hammer or rolling pin and give it a light pounding. You want to just break a bit of the structure of the veggies.

5. Sprinkle the salt over the vegetables, press a plate over the top of them, and then leave them for at least four hours.

6. Quarter the Asian pear and then mix that and the juniper berries in with the vegetables with your hand.

7. Place the mixture into your jar. This can get messy; I recommend doing this over your bowl.

8. Press down on your vegetables; if you need to add water to ensure they are submerged, then add some or all of the filtered water. Then place a weight over them and cover with a small piece of material or an airlock.

9. Place the whole jar in a spot that is warm (not hot) and away from direct sunlight and leave for two to seven days, preferably a little longer.

10. Once fermented, seal and leave in the refrigerator. Use within a few months.

Note: *A quick tip when it comes to peeling the ginger: peel the ginger skin by using the back of a teaspoon as if it were a pairing knife. Believe me, it works.*

Fermented Eggplant

YIELD: 2 quarts (2 L) eggplant   SUGGESTED JAR SIZE: two 1-quart (1-L) jars
PREP TIME: 1 hour   FERMENTATION TIME: 1 day

I first tried this recipe on a family holiday to Tuscany, Italy, where it was served as part of an antipasto platter. I found it went well with cured pork and other strong meats. Making your own fermented eggplant means that you can keep using the leftover oil to drizzle on pizza, pasta, or salads to give a bit of an extra flavor hit.

INGREDIENTS

2 cups (500 ml) filtered or unchlorinated water, plus more if needed

1 tablespoon sea salt

3 to 4 medium eggplants

2 medium bell peppers

1 tablespoon fresh oregano

¼ ounce (7 g) fresh thyme

2 teaspoons capers

10 small or 5 large pitted green olives, cut in half

2 tablespoons raw honey

1 medium bulb garlic

2 chili peppers

¼ cup Easy Apple Cider Vinegar (see page 92)

1 cup (250 ml) extra virgin olive oil, if needed

INSTRUCTIONS

1. Prepare the brine by boiling 1 cup of the water and stirring in the salt until dissolved and letting it cool. Boil just over 1 cup as you might lose a little due to the evaporation process. Allow it to cool.

2. Chop off the green tops of the eggplants, then peel and slice them. Your peeler will need to be very sharp to peel an eggplant, and you may have to resort to using a sharp knife. Cut the eggplant into ¾-inch-wide strips and place them straight into the brine to avoid discoloration.

3. Cut the tops off the bell peppers, slice in half, and deseed them before cutting them into ¼-inch-wide strips. Add these and the brine to your crock along with the oregano, thyme, capers, and olives.

4. Firmly but gently pound the vegetables inside the crock to help them release more liquid. Then place the small plate and the weights over them. You may decide to use a zip-top bag or two filled with water instead, and this will work very well too.

5. Leave the crock away from direct sunlight in your usual fermentation spot for 24 hours.

6. Drain the vegetables in a salad spinner or colander.

7. Boil the remaining 1 cup of water and stir in the honey; you may lose some due to evaporation, so top up with filtered or unchlorinated water if necessary. Allow to cool.

8. Peel and mince the garlic and chop up the chilies.

9. Using your hands, mix all the ingredients in a bowl, including the apple cider vinegar and honey water; this is a messy job—the squeamish may want to use a wooden spoon.

10. Transfer all to a 2-quart jar (or two 1-quart jars). You may need to top up with olive oil, depending on how much will fit in your jar. If using big eggplants, you might even find there is some overflow to an extra jar. Store in the refrigerator for up to a year.

Brined Garlic

YIELD: 1 pint (500 ml) garlic   SUGGESTED JAR SIZE: 1 pint (500 ml)
PREP TIME: 30 minutes to 1 hour   FERMENTATION TIME: 4 weeks

The lengthy preparation time in this recipe is due to the amount of garlic that you have to peel, which can get a little tedious. However, if you switch on the radio or chat with a friend while doing it, then the experience is transformed into a meditative and even enjoyable experience.

The results make the peeling worthwhile, because the fermented cloves are not as pungent as raw garlic, and so can make excellent additions to salads or antipasto plates.

You'll also notice there's a big variation in the number of garlic bulbs called for in this recipe; this is simply because garlic bulbs vary greatly in size.

INGREDIENTS

6 to 10 garlic bulbs
2 cups (500 ml) filtered or unchlorinated water
1 tablespoon sea salt

INSTRUCTIONS

1. Peel the papery bit off all of the garlic cloves and place them one by one into the jar.

2. Make the brine by boiling ¼ cup (60 ml) of the water, stirring in the salt until fully dissolved and then adding the rest of the water.

3. Pour the brine over the garlic, cover your jar with a small piece of material or an airlock, and leave out of direct sunlight for up to four weeks, ensuring that the cloves stay submerged in the water.

4. Keep an eye on them to make sure there are not any rogue cloves or that the water hasn't evaporated.

5. After the four weeks, transfer to the refrigerator and use within six months.

Note: *Don't be alarmed if any of your cloves turn blue, as this is due to the sulfur content in the garlic reacting with some of the enzymes and amino acids that are also present. It doesn't mean the garlic has gone moldy; it is still edible.*

Pickled Onions

YIELD: 1 quart (1 L) onions   SUGGESTED JAR SIZE: 1 quart (1 L)

PREP TIME: 5 to 10 minutes   FERMENTATION TIME: 3 to 5 days

Pearl onions are normal onions planted at high density and then picked early. If you are happy to wait, you can grow your own. Plant them outdoors during late winter or early spring and they should be ready to harvest in May.

The best use for pickled onions is to make a Gibson (cocktail), which is basically a martini with onions instead of olives. Pickled onions are also excellent on fatty foods. Try them in a grilled cheese sandwich!

INGREDIENTS

2 pounds (1 kg) pearl onions

2 to 4 cups (500 ml to 1 L) filtered or unchlorinated water

1 tablespoon sea salt

1 teaspoon peppercorns

1 tablespoon whole cloves

2 teaspoons black mustard seeds

1 bay leaf

1 tablespoon liquid from a previous ferment (if available)

INSTRUCTIONS

1. If your onions are still in their skins, then peel them. Don't overpeel bigger onions in order to get pearl onions, as most of the beneficial flavonoids are just below the surface of an onion.

2. Boil ½ cup of the water and stir in the sea salt until it has fully dissolved. Mix with the cooler filtered or unchlorinated water.

3. Put your spices into the bottom of the jar, then plop your onions on top of them. Pour over the brine solution. You can add a bit of the liquid from a previous ferment to help kick-start the process.

4. Place the weights over the onions to keep them submerged, and then loosely cover with a piece of material or an airlock jar to keep out flying critters. Keep out of direct sunlight for three to five days and allow to ferment.

5. Refrigerate and eat within six months to a year.

Turmeric and Celery

YIELD: 8 ounces (225 g) turmeric and celery
SUGGESTED JAR SIZE: 8 ounces (250 ml) if available, 1 pint (500 ml) if not
PREP TIME: 5 to 10 minutes   FERMENTATION TIME: 1 week

There is something odd about turmeric, in a good way. When I cook with it I notice what a huge difference a small amount can make for the color of a dish, but I rarely notice much of a difference in flavor. When fermented I notice a huge difference in flavor, and here it seems to even take over the taste of the celery.

Those who wish to take turmeric for health reasons will want to add the peppercorns. This is because the piperine in peppercorns helps you absorb the curcumin (the chemical that does you good) in turmeric by up to 2,000 percent.

INGREDIENTS

4 celery sticks (about 8 oz; 225 g)

1 inch fresh turmeric*

12 peppercorns (optional)

1 cup (250 ml) filtered or unchlorinated water

1 teaspoon sea salt

* Often sold as whole raw root

INSTRUCTIONS

1. Slice the celery into ribbons that are about ½ inch shorter than your jar. Grate the turmeric; you may wish to wear gloves for this job.

2. Pop the celery, turmeric, and peppercorns, if using, in the jar.

3. Make your brine by boiling ¼ cup of the water, then stirring in the salt, before topping up with the rest of the water. Allow to cool, then pour over the celery and turmeric.

4. Cover your jar with a small piece of material or an airlock and leave to ferment for one week.

5. Keep refrigerated and use within six months.

Lacto-Fermented Green Beans

YIELD: ½ pound (250 g) green beans   SUGGESTED JAR SIZE: 1 pint (500 ml)
PREP TIME: 5 to 10 minutes   INITIAL FERMENTATION TIME: 3 to 5 days
SECONDARY FERMENTATION TIME: 10 days

When planting your own green beans, it makes sense to plant as many as possible so that some will survive the ravishes of the inevitable slug attack. This was my own wise (or so I thought) approach to growing green beans. It worked well until we got a very dry year, and I ended up with my own body weight in green beans that all came ready at the same time. Had I had this recipe at the time it would have been a godsend!

I was alerted to the idea of fermenting beans when I read *Preserving Everything,* by the deeply talented Leda Meredith. She stated that it was one of the easiest recipes in her book. Indeed, I am hard pressed to think of another recipe that's easier.

INGREDIENTS

½ pound (250 g) green beans

1 cup (250 ml) filtered or unchlorinated water

1 tablespoon liquid from sauerkraut or another lacto-fermented vegetable (optional)

1 teaspoon sea salt

INSTRUCTIONS

1. Wash the beans. Nip off one end from all of them, then put a couple into the jar and cut off the tops so that they are ¼ inch below the neck of the jar. This will help you measure just how much you need to cut off the rest of them. Line the beans up to your "guide beans" and cut off the other end from the rest of them.

2. Make your brine by boiling ¼ cup of the water and mixing in the salt. Stir until fully dissolved before adding the rest of the water and allowing to cool.

3. Start stuffing the beans into your jar. It helps to turn the jar on its side.

4. Keep stuffing until they are wedged tighter than the New York subway.*

5. Turn the jar the right way up and pour in the salted water. Loosely fit the lid back on; in order for the culture to develop you'll need some air to come into contact with the beans and water. If you want to give it a little helping hand, then pour some liquid from a sauerkraut or another lacto-fermented vegetable.

6. Place the jar onto a saucer. Leave for three to five days at room temperature.

7. Keep an eye on the beans. You're looking for bubbles, a smell like sauerkraut, and a tangy taste.

8. When the beans have fermented for at least 24 hours, it's time to screw on the lid and put in the fridge.

9. Leave in the fridge for 10 days and then they are ready to eat. Eat within three months. They will start to discolor after this time but don't worry, they are still edible.

* Really tight.

Ukrainian Fermented Tomatoes

YIELD: 1 quart (1 L) tomatoes   SUGGESTED JAR SIZE: 1 quart (1 L)
PREP TIME: 15 minutes   FERMENTATION TIME: 3 to 7 days

I first found out about this style of tomato, popular in the Ukraine, while listening to a podcast featuring Olia Hercules, a food writer famed in the UK. It's hard to describe the flavor of this tomato to really do it justice, so I think I'll go along with Olia who enthusiastically describes them as "really tomatoey." After you taste them you'll realize just how perfect a description that is. I also asked my Latvian neighbor, Daiga, about them and found myself a new friend; we bonded over the tastes and joy of fermented foods. It would seem they are a delight known well across much of Eastern Europe.

Traditionally this ferment is made with dill, but this can be hard to come by in some areas. Instead, I swapped it out for basil. Some of the other flavorings in this ferment can also be swapped out and changed in accordance to your own taste. It might sound crazy, but because the tomato picks up and amplifies the flavors by the fermentation process, just be sure that you like all the herbs and spices that go in. Think of it like you are making a pasta sauce! If you are new to experimenting with flavors, then try it with just dill for the first time until you build up your confidence. It is also a great way to learn just how herbs enhance foods.

I've added these tomatoes to pizza and they are great, but some of the liquid needs to be squeezed out of them first. I've also made an interesting take on a Reuben sandwich with them using Sourdough Bread (page 169), Fermented Dilly "Cukes" (page 132), and Corned Beef (page 201). Use them for anything that requires a hit of tomato.

INGREDIENTS

6 medium tomatoes

2 to 3 cups (500 to 750 ml) filtered or unchlorinated water (depending on how much jar space your tomatoes take up)

1 to 2 tablespoons sea salt

1 bay leaf

A few sprigs basil

10 to 20 peppercorns

Optional extras: 5 garlic cloves (peeled), 1 allspice berry, 2 whole cloves, a large horseradish leaf, blackcurrant leaf

INSTRUCTIONS

1. Prick the tomatoes at the top using a fork; I pushed the fork right in up to the top of the prongs, as this helps to stop the tomatoes from splitting. It will also allow the lovely lacto goodness to get right inside them.

2. Make your brine by boiling ¼ cup of the water, stirring in the salt until fully dissolved, and then topping up with the rest of the water. Cool before use.

3. Pop the bay leaf, basil, peppercorns, and optional items, if using, in the bottom of the jar.

4. Add the tomatoes and brine to the jar and close the lid.

5. Leave for at least three to seven days. The first time I made this I found that the usual three days wasn't long enough to really get a fizzy tomato and instead needed to leave mine for a week.

6. Once the tomatoes have fermented, move them to the refrigerator and eat within a year.

Potato Cheese

YIELD: 1 pound (500 g) potato cheese   SUGGESTED FERMENTATION VESSEL: crock
PREP TIME: 2 minutes   FERMENTATION TIME: 3 days for soft cheese, 16 days for harder cheese

Traditionally, potato cheese is made with "clobbered" milk, that is, raw milk that has been left to sour. Unfortunately, you can't make the same thing with store-bought milk left out, because the pasteurization process will have killed off any of the enzymes that help it ferment. You can instead use kefir (see recipe, page 254), which works as a more-than-adequate substitute.

Be warned that this is a strong-tasting "cheese," so if you are used to a bland Cheddar, then I'd perhaps skip this recipe. If, on the other hand, you are a cheese addict, then you will welcome it as a cheaper alternative to some of the strong European cheeses. Adapting the recipe to use coconut milk kefir means that even those who have dietary restrictions with dairy can enjoy this cheese.

INGREDIENTS

1 pound (500 g) potatoes

1 cup (250 ml) kefir or clobbered milk

1½ teaspoons sea salt

INSTRUCTIONS

1. Wash, peel, and cut up the potatoes into bite-sized chunks. (Those who enjoy zero-waste cooking might want to try frying the skins in a little butter and some spices for a tasty snack.)

2. Boil or steam the peeled potatoes until they are soft. Then allow them to cool to room temperature.

3. Next, mash the potatoes; they can be either thrown into a food processor along with the kefir and salt or passed through a potato ricer and then mixed with the kefir and salt or mashed with a masher, mixing in the kefir and salt. Whichever method you choose, make sure that your mash has a smooth consistency without any lumps.

4. Place the mashed potatoes into your crock. It is essential that you cover your crock, plastic wrap works well, especially if making this during the warmer months. Fruit flies seem to love it, and they seem able to find their way through loose material covers.

5. Once covered leave in your usual fermentation spot out of direct sunlight for two days.

6. After two days strain the cheese. Wrap it in a length of cheesecloth and tie it to a door handle on a kitchen cupboard and let it drip down into a bowl. You could also try tying a spoon to the muslin cloth and letting it hang over a jug. However you drain yours, keep it draining until the dripping stops. When it finishes you'll have potato cheese, and it can be eaten at this point. It's quite strange and essentially tastes like sour mashed potatoes.

7. For a harder "cheese" that can be used to flavor dishes or shaved over pasta, instead of stopping the fermentation process on the third day, stir in the content's surface mold. This helps to inoculate the rest of the potatoes from spreading the spores throughout the medium. You can then leave it for an additional week.

8. The "cheese" is then ready to be made into patties by rolling into a 1-inch (3-cm) round ball, then flattening. Place your patties on a wire rack, covering them with a tea towel. Place the wire rack somewhere with good air circulation and leave them for an additional week. They are ready when they are hard and don't contain any moisture.

9. Once done, leave in the refrigerator wrapped with some parchment paper and use within a year.

Note: *Mashing potatoes with kefir and salt is a tasty dish in and of itself.*

Fermented Dilly "Cukes"

YIELD: 1 pint (500 ml) "cukes"   SUGGESTED JAR SIZE: 1 pint (500 ml)
PREP TIME: 3 minutes   FERMENTATION TIME: 5 days to 2 weeks

I am sure I am not alone in thinking that the perfect sandwich contains a bit of pickled cucumber.

This recipe is for a pint of cukes. If your mini cucumbers are a little less than mini, you could double, triple, or quadruple the measurements to make more.

The best time to shop for mini "cukes" is in the summer when they should be growing in abundance. You can adapt this recipe by adding your own spice mix to your "cukes" but avoid using any powdered spices, as these tend to float to the top and are a big invitation for a mold party.

INGREDIENTS

2 cups (500 ml) filtered or unchlorinated water

1 tablespoon sea salt

2 garlic cloves

1 large sprig of dill

1 teaspoon peppercorns

1 leaf of either grape, blackberry, oak, or horseradish

5 to 6 small, firm cucumbers (about 4 oz; 120 g each) or half a large cucumber sliced into quarters

INSTRUCTIONS

1. Boil 1 cup of the water and stir in the salt until dissolved, top up with the rest of the water, and then allow to cool.

2. Peel and lightly crush the garlic cloves and drop one into your jar along with half the dill, peppercorns, and a leaf of your choosing.

3. Pack in the cucumbers one by one. The bigger ones work best at the bottom. At about halfway up put in the rest of the dill and the garlic and continue to layer up, leaving around an inch of headspace at the very top. If using chopped cucumbers, place half of the slices in the jar, add the dill and garlic, then add the rest.

4. Pour the brine over the cucumbers, popping a weight over them to make sure they don't rise above the waterline. Cover with a small square of material or an airlock.

5. Leave the jar in your usual fermentation spot (out of sunlight and at room temperature) for a minimum of five days and up to two or three weeks, depending on how sour you wish yours to be.

6. Once they have reached your optimum level of tastiness, return the lid to the jar and pop in the refrigerator for up to six months, but in all reality they should last for longer.

Crunchy Carrots

YIELD: 1 quart (1 L) carrots   SUGGESTED JAR SIZE: 1 quart (1 L)

PREP TIME: 3 to 10 minutes   FERMENTATION TIME: 7 to 10 days

This recipe will work with all carrots. At one time I only used carrots that had been cut up to bâtonnet size or baby carrots that come washed and peeled in bags at the supermarket. If these are all you can get, then don't hesitate to use them. As an experiment I decided to use bigger, normal-sized carrots whole. I was delighted with the results. They come out wonderfully fizzy and tangy. They work great when served on the side of a plate or when grated as part of a salad, especially with some Easy Plum Vinegar (page 94) drizzled over them.

Another favorite of mine is to use mixed baby rainbow carrots. Their vibrant purples, yellows, and whites look so inviting when sitting in the fermenting jars. Rainbow carrots can be difficult to find, and in some areas you might even be better off trying to grow your own. We grow carrots on the windowsill in my daughter's tiny bedroom. I say this to illustrate how they need not take up much space. They can indeed be grown in a small window box, even in the smallest of apartments. If growing really isn't for you, then I'd suggest searching for them at a specialty fruit and vegetable store or at farmers' markets.

Once fermented, all the carrots are delicious and to my taste, as they take on a hint of smoky bacon!

INGREDIENTS

2 cups baby carrots or enough large carrots to fill a quart jar

2 cups (500 ml) filtered or unchlorinated water

1 tablespoon sea salt

INSTRUCTIONS

1. Rinse the carrots. You don't want to get rid of any helpful bacteria, so don't be too vigilant, but neither do you want to have any grit or mud on your finished product. If using full-sized carrots, then you can either chop them to fit your jar or slice into chunks depending on preference.

2. Boil ½ cup of the water and stir in the salt until it has fully dissolved. Top up with the rest of the water to make 2 cups.

3. Place the carrots into your jar and pour over the brine. I tend to use a weight to weigh mine down, as they can get quite buoyant. Cover with a small piece of material or an airlock.

4. Leave in a dark and warmish spot to ferment for a week to 10 days, then refrigerate. They should keep for up to a year, but perhaps even longer in reality.

Sauerkraut

YIELD: 1 quart (1 L) sauerkraut   SUGGESTED JAR SIZE: 1 quart (1 L)

PREP TIME: 15 minutes   SALTING TIME: 4 to 12 hours   FERMENTATION TIME: 3 days to 2 weeks

I was first introduced to sauerkraut at college, when I shared a house with an actual Hamburger (a person from Hamburg, Germany). I fell in love with the stuff, especially when eating German sausages. I must have spent a good portion of my student loan on it. It never dawned on me that I could have made my own and saved a fortune. Moreover, the homemade version can be tailored to your own tastes. I like it with juniper berries and caraway seeds. This gives it an extra burst of flavor with each bite.

INGREDIENTS

1 small cabbage

1 teaspoon caraway seeds (optional)

Up to 40 juniper berries (optional)

1 to 2 tablespoons sea salt, plus 1 tablespoon more if needed

2 cups (500 ml) filtered or unchlorinated water, if needed

INSTRUCTIONS

1. Quarter the cabbage and cut out the core. You can cut up the core into tiny chunks and it gives a little crunch and sweetness to the final ferment or you can discard it. Cut or grate your cabbage into thin ribbons.

2. Chuck the cabbage into a large bowl and massage in the caraway seeds and juniper berries (if using) and salt. Traditionally, children would have walked on great tubs of sliced cabbage at this stage, and you could upscale and do the same!

   I'd suggest instead pounding with the back of a wooden spoon or rolling pin. This helps to break down the cell walls. I find this stage very satisfying, as you hear that crunch of cabbage breaking.

3. Leave the bowl for at least 4 hours and up to 12. The salt will help to draw out the liquid from the cabbage. If there isn't enough liquid to cover the cabbage after four hours, you can always add your own brine by mixing 1 tablespoon of salt per 1 pint (500 ml) water and then using what you need.

4. Transfer the cabbage to your jar.

5. Weigh down the cabbage so that none is poking out of the brine. Leave for a minimum of three days in hot weather. I like to leave mine for at least five days and up to two weeks for a more tangy, flavorsome kraut. I have heard of people leaving theirs for over a month. It's all a matter of taste. So just keep tasting it and when you personally like the flavor and think it's done, then it's done.

6. Put the lid back on and refrigerate. It will keep for around six months.

Note: *On a personal note, I always found macaroni and cheese to sit rather uncomfortably in my gut. Stirring in some sauerkraut seems to help me digest it.*

Pickled Squash/Pumpkin

YIELD: 1 quart (1 L) squash/pumpkin   SUGGESTED JAR SIZE: 1 quart (1 L)
PREP TIME: 10 to 20 minutes   FERMENTATION TIME: 1 week

I studied a number of approaches before I settled on this recipe—some add more or less spices, all suggest a short fermentation time, and none recommend adding whey (as many older recipe books suggest) or using a bit of starter from a previous ferment. This latter advice is because a starter can cause the ferment to happen a little too quickly, causing mush in a jar. My Latvian neighbor, Daiga, suggests fermenting whole squashes and pumpkins picked off the plant when still small, around the size of a fist.

I am partial to adding just a bit of cinnamon in this ferment, but you don't have to stop there.

Warming spices work very well when paired with squashes. Just be mindful about the amplification effect of fermentation—overload your jar and you'll overload your final product. On a cautionary note, don't use powdered spices as these will float to the top of your jar and attract mold spores.

INGREDIENTS

16 ounces (450 g) peeled squash (save a few pieces unpeeled)

One 2- to 3-inch (5- to 7-cm) cinnamon stick

Other recommended spice additions: 3 to 5 whole cloves, 1 whole nutmeg, 2 inches (5 cm) fresh ginger, sliced

3 cups (750 ml) filtered or unchlorinated water

1 tablespoon sea salt

INSTRUCTIONS

1. Peel and dice the squash. This can be a tricky process. I recommend slicing it in half, or even quarters, before peeling by cutting just below the skin with a very sharp knife. As beneficial bacteria live on the skin of fruit and vegetables, keep a few unpeeled chunks—just remember to cut off the peel once fermented.

2. Put the spice(s) into the bottom of your jar and then stack the squash on top of it.

3. Make your brine by boiling ¼ cup of water, stirring in the salt until fully dissolved, and then topping up with the rest of the water. Cool before pouring over your squash.

4. Cover loosely with a piece of material or attach an airlock and leave to ferment for approximately one week.

5. After that time, pick out the chunks of pumpkin or squash with the skin still on and peel them. I find the ferment is more likely to mold if you leave them on.

6. Once fermented, keep refrigerated and use within a month.

Broccoli Stems

YIELD: 1 pint (500 ml) broccoli stems   SUGGESTED JAR SIZE: 1 quart (1 L)
PREP TIME: 5 minutes   FERMENTATION TIME: 4 to 5 days

This recipe helps to use up any leftover stems of broccoli. It works equally as well with purple-sprouting broccoli as it does with regular broccoli. Try to use crisp stems and not ones that have gone a little limp.

The recipe can be altered to your tastes by adding different herbs and spices. I have suggested some, but you might also want to use garlic, peppercorns, a bay leaf, or other whole herbs and spices of your choosing.

INGREDIENTS

2 cups (500 ml) filtered or unchlorinated water

2 teaspoons sea salt

2 pounds (4 kg) broccoli stems

1 teaspoon sliced fresh ginger and/or turmeric root

½ chili (optional)

INSTRUCTIONS

1. Boil ½ cup of the water and stir in the salt until fully dissolved, then top up with the rest of the water and put to one side.

2. Cut off the stems of the broccoli as far up to the florets as possible. If you are not going to be cooking the florets that day, store in the crisper section of your refrigerator; they also benefit from being inside another container with a few holes to let the broccoli breathe. I sometimes peel the stems with a peeler, as it makes them slightly more tender when

fermented, but this is optional. The first time you make this, peel some stems and leave others so that you have an idea of your preference.

3. Place the ginger and/or the turmeric root and the chili (if using) into the clean jar.

4. Push the stems into the jar one by one; the last few might have to be stuffed in. Pour in the brine.

Ensure that there are none poking out over the water, and cut to fit as needed.

5. Cover your jar with a piece of material or add an airlock, then place in a warm spot out of direct sunlight for four to five days. Once fermented, refrigerate and use within around six months.

Fermented Swiss Chard Stems

YIELD: 1 quart (1 L) swiss chard stems   SUGGESTED JAR SIZE: 1 quart (1 L)
PREP TIME: 20 minutes   FERMENTATION TIME: 3 to 5 days

Rainbow chard is really easy to grow; it doesn't need much attention and yet it will reward you with a splash of color in those drab months.

This recipe makes a delicious and nutritious use of the fleshy stems that might otherwise go to compost. Approximately two large bunches of chard stems are used here.

I find that the taste of the stems intensify when fermented. It offers some freshness akin to the last clutch of winter turning into springtime.

INGREDIENTS

2½ cups (625 ml) filtered or unchlorinated water

1½ teaspoons sea salt

11 ounces (300 g) Swiss chard stems (enough to fill a jar)

INSTRUCTIONS

1. Make up the brine by boiling ½ cup (125 ml) of the water and stirring the salt into it until it is dissolved. Then top up with the rest of the water to cool.

2. Slice off the ends of all the chard stems. Depending on where and how it is grown, your chard might not have very big stems; in which case, you may wish to cut around the leaf from the central mid-rib and use that too.

3. Cut one piece, then pop it in a quart jar and try it out for size, ensuring that it fits standing upright and that there is about 1 inch (3 cm) of space at the top. You can then measure the rest of your chard alongside that one piece. Turn the jar on its side and keep popping in your perfectly cut stems one by one. You'll have to jam in the last few.

4. Once the jar is full, pour over the brine, cover with a small piece of material or an airlock, and leave on the countertop to ferment for three to five days. If the stems are tightly packed, there is no need to weigh them down, but keep an eye on them in case a rogue one tries to makes its escape.

5. After a few days you should see some bubbles forming amongst the stems. Taste a stem and if it has a tang to it, put them in the fridge. I can't resist and will eat them straightaway, but they are better after a couple of weeks.

6. Keep refrigerated and use within six months.

Fermented Vine Leaves

YIELD: 2 pints (1 L) vine leaves   SUGGESTED JAR SIZE: two 1-pint (500-ml) jars
PREP TIME: 1 hour (will shorten with practice)   FERMENTATION TIME: 2 weeks

I planted a grapevine in our backyard four years ago. Alas, I have never made wine with these grapes because the snails seem to get the fruit before it's time to harvest! Determined to get some kind of harvest from it, I started to harvest the abundant leaves instead. The result was delicious, perfect for making stuffed vine leaves.

When harvesting the leaves, opt for ones that are free of any blemishes and insect damage. I also prefer the leaves that are slightly shielded from direct sunlight. Therefore, I go for the ones that grow beneath the larger, thicker leaves. The best leaves can be harvested at any point from late spring to early summer. The leaves on the vine continue to grow throughout the season, and you'll still be able to pick them until the grapes have been harvested. You can harvest leaves from wild grapevines, but don't overpick a vine. You want to be sure the plant will continue to thrive in subsequent seasons. To pick your vine leaves, either pull the stem off the leaf or cut them off with a pair of scissors or snips.

If making stuffed vine leaves seems like too much of a chore, don't worry; fermented vine leaves do have other uses! First, they can be used to enhance your other pickles and ferments. Simply drape one over the top of the produce in your pickle jar. The tannins from the leaf have the added benefit of keeping your vegetables crisp. Second, you can also add fermented vine leaves to stocks and stews to give them a bit of body and flavor.

This recipe is the right size to preserve all the leaves from one out-of-control grapevine. If yours produces less or more, you can adjust accordingly.

INGREDIENTS

4 cups (1 qt; 1 L) filtered or unchlorinated water

2 tablespoons sea salt

60 to 80 vine leaves

INSTRUCTIONS

1. Make your brine by boiling ¼ cup of the water, stirring in the salt until fully dissolved, and then topping up with the rest of the water. Cool before use.

2. Next, stack the vine leaves into piles of 20. It's advisable to do this in size order with the largest at the bottom and the smallest at the top—but you don't have to be too exacting. Roll up or fold your vine leaves and place half into each 1-pint (500-ml) jar. Depending on your jars you can either place them in lengthwise or flat. Be careful not to tear any leaves as you place them in.

3. Pour the brine over the vine leaves and wrap one vine leaf over the top of your bundles in order to keep the rest submerged.

4. Cover with a small piece of material, secured with a rubber band or an airlock, then place in a warm spot for two weeks and then refrigerate. They will keep for up to a year; after that they start to taste a little too funky.

Sauerruben

YIELD: 1 quart (1 L) sauerruben   SUGGESTED JAR SIZE: 1 quart (1 L)
PREP TIME: 20 minutes   FERMENTATION TIME: 3 to 5 days

When I was growing up it was difficult to come by anything but brassicas and root vegetables during the winter months. Finding a different use for a turnip would have been a godsend. It was a shame I didn't know about this recipe then. This is a turnip like you have never tasted before.

INGREDIENTS

4 cups (1 L) filtered or unchlorinated water

2 tablespoons sea salt

8 turnips (about 16 lb; 7.2 kg)

1 fresh hot chili pepper (optional)

INSTRUCTIONS

1. Make up the brine by boiling ½ cup of the water, then stirring in the sea salt until fully dissolved. Top up with the rest of the water and put to one side.

2. Cut off the tops and bottoms, then peel and slice the turnips. There are a few different ways in which you can cut the turnips, depending on how you like your sauerruben. I personally like to grate mine, but they can be cut into thin, round sections or sliced julienne style.

3. Cut the chili pepper in half and pop it in the jar.

4. Place the turnip slices or grated turnip into your jar and pour over the brine, pushing down on them to ensure there are no trapped bubbles.

5. Add a weight on top to keep the turnips submerged under the waterline.

6. Cover with a small piece of material secured with a rubber band or an airlock, then place in a warm spot for three to five days until they have fermented. You can leave for longer, depending on your preference.

7. After they have fermented to your desired sourness, move to the refrigerator and use within six months.

Note: *Did you know that turnip leaves are edible? Steam them and melt a little butter on them, or even try fermenting them in their own right.*

Fermented Carolina-Style Coleslaw

YIELD: 1 quart (1 L) coleslaw   SUGGESTED JAR SIZE: 1 quart (1 L)
PREP TIME: 2 hours 30 minutes   FERMENTATION TIME: 3 to 7 days

Coleslaw is a Dutch invention that literally means *cabbage salad.* Therefore, strictly speaking, you can't make coleslaw if you don't include at least some cabbage. This Carolina-style slaw may differ from any you have tasted before, because it is soured by fermentation rather than vinegar. According to a number of sources, it is probably very close to the original thing.

What constitutes Carolina style can cause huge arguments among North and South Carolinians; the caveat is that this recipe can be adapted to every person's preferences. Add a thinly sliced onion, add more mustard—it is up to you. You can even swap out the green cabbage for a Napa cabbage or use a red cabbage if you wish. You might have to call it something else, however, if you serve it to a Carolinian!

With some trepidation I feel I should weigh in and say that, to me, a good Carolina-style slaw must contain mustard seeds. Adding them before you start fermenting helps to enhance and infuse the flavor throughout the slaw.

Serve with chili dogs, hamburgers, or bring along to the next cookout and share with as many people as will eat it.

INGREDIENTS

1 pound (500 g) green cabbage
1 green bell pepper (about 8 oz; 200 g)
1 carrot (about 5 oz; 100 g)
½ celery root (about 5 oz; 100 g)
1 tablespoon sea salt
2 teaspoons yellow mustard seeds
¼ cup (80 g) honey
½ cup olive oil
Twist of ground black pepper

INSTRUCTIONS

1. Cut or grate the cabbage into small ribbons and place this in a deep mixing bowl. Cut the bell pepper in half, then slice into small chunks. Peel and grate the carrot and celery root and add them to the bowl.

2. Sprinkle over the sea salt and mustard seeds and then pound the mixture until you start to see some liquid coming from the cabbage. Place a plate over the top of the cabbage and press down. Leave for a couple of hours as this will help with the extraction of water.

3. Transfer the slaw to your jar and cover loosely with a small piece of material and a rubber band and leave in your usual fermentation spot out of direct sunlight to ferment for three to seven days until your desired sourness has been achieved.

4. Next, drain off the liquid from the ferment and transfer it to a mixing bowl. Stir in the honey and the oil, then transfer back into your jar and place back in the refrigerator. Use within a month or two, although it will keep for longer.

Passilla Chili Daikon

YIELD: 1 quart (1 L) daikon   SUGGESTED JAR SIZE: 1 quart (1 L)
PREP TIME: 5 to 10 minutes   FERMENTATION TIME: 1 to 4 weeks, depending on preference

Passillas are a milder chili pepper with a somewhat earthy flavor—they don't have the heat like some chilies do. To my taste, this means they are the ideal partner for the daikon radish, which doesn't have the kick of a conventional red radish.

INGREDIENTS

1 pound (500 g) daikon radishes

1 to 2 tablespoons pasilla chili flakes (or one pasilla chili, toasted and flaked)

1 tablespoon sea salt

2 cups (500 ml) filtered or unchlorinated water

INSTRUCTIONS

1. Rinse any mud and grit off the radish, then slice up into thumb-sized pieces.

2. Stuff the radishes into the jar and sprinkle over the chili flakes.

3. Make up your brine by dissolving the salt in the water. You can boil a small amount of the water and stir in the salt before topping up with the rest of the colder water.

4. Ensure that the brine is at least room temperature if not cool, then pour it into the jar and weigh down the contents. Cover with a small piece of material or an airlock.

5. Leave the jar somewhere it won't be disturbed to ferment for one to four weeks. The length of time will depend on how tangy you like your ferments to be. Refrigerate and use within six months.

Beet Kvass

YIELD: 1 pint (500 ml) kvass   SUGGESTED JAR SIZE: 1 quart (1 L)

PREP TIME: 5 to 10 minutes   FERMENTATION TIME: 7 to 14 days

Beet kvass is becoming a popular global drink, helped of course by food bloggers and authors. I got this recipe from Emily Han, a Los Angeles–based author and naturalist. It's a very straightforward and rather easy recipe to follow.

Beet kvass isn't anything like bread kvass (see Kvass, page 186). There is something of the earth about it, and this comes from the beets. It is also sour, salty, and in this author's opinion, delicious.

INGREDIENTS

2 ounces (340 g) beets

4 cups (1 L) filtered or unchlorinated water

1 to 2 teaspoons sea salt

Optional add-ins: 1 inch fresh ginger, 1 cinnamon stick, 3 to 4 whole cloves, or lemon or orange slices

INSTRUCTIONS

1. Trim off the tops and tails of the beets but leave the skins on. Scrub off any dirt or soil.

2. Cut the beets into ½-inch cubes. It is not necessary to cut precise shapes and sizes; you just want to give the beets enough surface area to ferment. Avoid finely chopping or grating the beets, which can lead to very rapid fermentation and alcohol production—unless of course you want that!

3. Place the beets in a very clean, but never soapy, 1-quart (1-L) jar.

4. Boil your water, then stir in the salt until it dissolves. If you wish, you can also add your flavorings now, like ginger, a few slices of lemon or orange, a cinnamon stick, or a few cloves. Allow the brine to cool, then pour over the beets, leaving at least 1 inch (3 cm) of headspace at the top of the jar.

5. Cover the jar with a small piece of material or an airlock. You can also seal the jar if you wish, but you will need to check on it to ensure it doesn't blow! (See step 7.)

6. Let the jar stand at room temperature. You may see bubbles inside the jar, and brine may seep out of the lid; place a bowl or plate under the jar to help catch any overflow.

7. If you have sealed the jar, open it once a day to taste the liquid and to release gases produced during fermentation. If any mold or scum has formed on the top, simply skim it off.

8. When it tastes strong enough for your liking, strain out the beets and transfer the kvass to the refrigerator. You may drink it right away, but it benefits from a few days conditioning in the refrigerator. As a fermented beverage, this kvass will last for about a month.

9. To make another batch of kvass, leave a little brine in the jar with the beets, add a teaspoon of salt, fill with water, and proceed as before. Second and third batches can be made this way, though they will taste weaker than the first. I'd suggest that you stop at two. The boldness of flavor has been lost by the time you get to a third run. The beets can then be used to make a rather salty borscht or just composted. This recipe can be easily doubled for a half-gallon jar or quadrupled for a gallon jar.

Ginger Beer

YIELD: 1 gallon (4.5 L) ginger beer   SUGGESTED FERMENTATION VESSEL: 1-gallon (4.5-L) carboy/demijohn
PREP TIME: 20 minutes, plus a few moments a day to make the bug
INITIAL FERMENTATION TIME: 24 to 72 hours   SECONDARY FERMENTATION TIME: 2 weeks

Ginger beer has been around for centuries. One typical old recipe dates back to 1815 and was found in a letter to the editor of *The Monthly Magazine*. It was written by T. Rayner of Brighton (southern England), who stated:

> Powder of ginger 1 ounce of tartar half an ounce a large sliced 2 1b lump sugar and one of water added together and over the fire for half an hour fermented in the usual way with a spoonful of yeast and bottle it for use. It may be proper to observe that it should be put in such bottles as are used for soda water and corked.

I might disagree with the 19th-century T. Rayner of Brighton in that I prefer to use grated fresh ginger when available rather than powdered. The powdered form does have an intense ginger flavor, but it is hotter than its fresh counterpart. Harsher would be an accurate description too. There is something more mellow and wholesome about using fresh ginger. Also, when making the initial bug (fermented ginger and sugar), fresh ginger seems to take much more quickly than powdered ginger, due to the extra bacteria and yeast cells already living on it.

As a matter of note, T. Rayner also mentions the use of tartar—many old recipes do. I presume what's meant here is potassium bitartrate, also known as cream of tartar, which is an anticaking, anticrystallizing agent with a strong flavor. I'd suggest that unless you want to keep your ginger beer for a long time or are fond of the tartar flavor, then it is a superfluous ingredient.

To make ginger beer you don't really need much more than some sugar and some ginger. When it comes to harvesting the wild yeast, it of course helps if you don't live in a yeast desert. Those living in high-rise city apartments might struggle with yeast. Simply put, these are places with little or no yeast cells in the air. Therefore, if your bug doesn't take after a few attempts, then use a packet of champagne yeast to get your ginger beer started. Alternatively, you can move it to the ground floor of your building or even take it to a friend's house until it starts to fizz.

INGREDIENTS

For the bug

1 cup (250 ml) filtered or unchlorinated water

Up to 12 teaspoons grated fresh ginger (about 2½ oz; 71 g)

Up to 12 teaspoons sugar (2½ oz; 71 g)

For the ginger beer

1 gallon (4.5 L) water

1 ounce (28 g) fresh ginger

1 pound (500 g) granulated sugar

2 lemons

1½ teaspoons cream of tartar (optional)

INSTRUCTIONS

1. For the bug: Pour 1 cup water into a 1-pint (500-ml) jar. Stir in 2 teaspoons of the grated ginger and the same amount of sugar, cover with a tea towel, and leave somewhere that keeps an even temperature in the range of 70 to 80°F (21 to 26°C).

2. Feed your bug 2 teaspoons each of sugar and grated ginger daily until it starts to froth. It can take up to two weeks for your bug to start, so be patient. To be on the safe side, don't use until it has been frothy for at least 36 hours.

3. For the ginger beer: Boil 1 gallon of the water. Smash the ginger with a rolling pin or mallet. You may wish to roll it up in a thick tea towel to stop your kitchen from getting splattered. Drop the smashed ginger into the pan of water and stir in the sugar.

4. Juice and peel the lemons and plop the peels into the pot too. Allow to boil for an additional 10 minutes.

5. Take off the heat, add the remaining water, and allow to cool to room temperature, around 70°F (22°C) before adding the juice of the lemons and the ginger bug. I recommend using a thermometer if you have one.

continued

6. Leave to ferment for 24 to 72 hours. Give it a shorter time in warmer states and longer in cooler states or in very well air-conditioned dwellings.

7. Strain out the lemon peel and ginger and pour the liquid into a 1-gallon (4.5-L) sterilized carboy/demijohn. Affix an airlock and leave for another two weeks.

8. After two weeks, siphon into sterilized bottles, then chill and serve. It goes well with melon slices or you might be tempted to serve just as the British do, complete with cucumber sandwiches with the crusts cut off. I also find ginger beer goes well with barbecued food.

Note: You may wonder why ginger is in the vegetable section of the supermarket. It's there because ginger is not a root but a rhizome, which, like a potato or yam, is actually the underground stem of the plant.

Turmeric and Cardamom "Beer"

YIELD: 1 gallon (4.5 L) turmeric and cardamom beer
SUGGESTED FERMENTATION VESSEL: 1 gallon (4.5 L) carboy/demijohn
PREP TIME: 2 hours, over a period of days   FERMENTATION TIME: 24 to 72 hours

Turmeric is from the same family as ginger. This gave me the idea to make a turmeric drink that is fermented in the same way as ginger beer, using a bug (fermented turmeric and sugar). I was pleased with the result. It is a very refreshing, mellow drink with hints of subtropical Asia.

I followed the recipe for Ginger Beer (page 154), with turmeric being swapped out for the ginger. The turmeric on its own is a little too earthy for my tastes, and so I added some cardamom and some lemons. These additional ingredients makes the earthiness a background flavor rather than a foreground flavor.

INGREDIENTS

For the bug

1 cup (250 ml) filtered or unchlorinated water
Up to 12 tablespoons grated turmeric (2½ oz; 71 g)
Up to 12 tablespoons sugar (2½ oz; 71 g)

For the turmeric beer

1 gallon (4.5 L) filtered or unchlorinated water
1 ounce (28 g) turmeric root
1 pound (500 g) granulated sugar
2 lemons
Pinch of ground black peppercorns
Pinch of cardamom seeds
Optional add-ins: 2 cinnamon sticks, 1 bay leaf, 1 tablespoon pink peppercorns

continued

INSTRUCTIONS

1. For the bug: Pour 1 cup of water into a 16-ounce (500 ml) jar.

2. Stir in 2 teaspoons each of the grated turmeric and the sugar, cover with a tea towel, and leave somewhere that keeps an even temperature in the range of 70 to 80°F (21 to 26°C).

3. Feed your bug 2 teaspoons each of sugar and grated turmeric daily until it starts to froth. It can take up to two weeks for the bug to start, so be patient. To be on the safe side, don't use until it has been frothy for at least 36 hours.

4. For the turmeric beer: Boil 2 quarts (2 L) of the water, and then smash the turmeric root with a rolling pin, mallet, or with the wide part of a meat cleaver; hard and direct force have the best results. Add this to the pan of water along with the 1 pound (500 g) of sugar.

5. Peel and juice the lemons and plop the peels into the pot, along with the peppercorns and cardamom. Allow to boil for an additional 10 minutes. If you wish to experiment, you can add more spices at this stage too, such as cinnamon sticks, a bay leaf, or pink peppercorns.

6. Take off the heat, add the remaining water, and allow to cool to room temperature, around 70°F (22°C) before adding the juice of the lemons and the turmeric bug. I recommend using a thermometer if you have one.

7. Place in a clean container with a loose cover or tea towel over it.

8. Leave in an area with a consistent temperature of 75 to 80°F (23 to 26°C) to ferment for 24 to 72 hours. The length of time will vary depending on room temperature. What you are looking for is the initial fermentation to calm down a little. Once it has stopped bubbling so much, then move on to the next step. Please note, you can go below this temperature, but I recommend not letting it be too far above as it will bring in off flavors.

9. You can bottle straightaway at this point, and to do so you'll need to siphon into bottles, leaving the sediment behind. You can certainly use flip-top bottles as they are designed to ping open; however, your turmeric beer could still be rather volatile, although (oddly) I find it often less volatile than the ginger beer made in the same way, so I tend to strain it into a sterilized carboy, affixing an airlock before leaving it for an additional two weeks, and then I siphon into bottles.

CHAPTER 5

Breads, Grains, and Pulses

The civilized world was built on grains. When we started farming them we needed to store them, and so small settlements started to appear around our grain storage areas. From these simple settlements, towns and later cities arose.

Grains are still vitally important. Breads, grains, and pulses make up about 90 percent of the world's diet, and for many people it is how the day is started. From a slice of toast or a bowl of cereal in the West to idlis in South India and ogi in Nigeria, Africa, we all want to fill our bellies before we start the day.

This chapter puts you in touch with the flavors of multiple cultures, and the recipes here are perhaps the most fun and hands-on in this book. I do hope you enjoy experimenting with these recipes as much as I did.

Fermented Mung Bean Pancakes

YIELD: Four or five 6-inch pancakes   SUGGESTED JAR SIZE: 1 pint (500 ml)
PREP TIME: 40 minutes, plus 6 to 8 hours soaking time   FERMENTATION TIME: 12 hours

This recipe has been adapted from one that came to me via the website Goodness Is (goodnessis.com). This inspirational website is by two sisters who live on either side of the globe and keep in contact through food. They state that the recipe came from their friend Lulu and that she is unsure of its origins. It is similar in nature to a Korean dish known as *bindaetteok*, as it uses mung beans, although this version contains no meat, egg, or many of the other things in traditional *bindaettok*.

The resulting pancakes are very tasty. I made my first batch with the intention of sharing with my family, and then proceeded to eat them all myself. The taste has hints of freshly podded peas and is an ideal accompaniment to an Indian meal.

INGREDIENTS

1 cup (6 oz; 175 g) mung beans
1 cup (250 ml) filtered or unchlorinated water
½ teaspoon sea salt
2 garlic cloves
1 teaspoon cumin seeds
½ teaspoon black mustard seeds
¼ teaspoon turmeric powder
1 ounce (30 g) fresh cilantro or coriander, finely chopped
A little butter or ghee for frying

INSTRUCTIONS

1. Leave the mung beans to soak in a bowl or jug with at least 2 cups of water for six to eight hours. After this time they will have swelled in size and become soft; I like to crunch on one to check, and if they are not soft they are not ready.

2. Drain off the water. Return to the bowl and, using a hand blender or food processor, blend together while slowly adding approximately 1 cup of the filtered water until it has become a thick pulp.

3. Stir in the salt, cover, and leave until you start to
    see bubbles. The batter should rise. If you don't see
    either happening, then you will need to move your
    batter to a warmer spot. It should take roughly
    12 hours to get to this state.

4. Mince or finely chop the garlic cloves and heat
    a frying pan or skillet until very hot. Drop in the
    garlic and seeds into the dry pan and toast. After
    two to five minutes, the mustard seeds will start
    jumping out of the pan, a surefire indication that
    they are ready.

5. Now pound the seeds and garlic in a mortar and
    pestle before adding to the mung bean pancake
    mixture or add them whole, depending on how
    adverse you are to the texture of seeds in your
    food.

6. Stir the turmeric and cilantro into the mixture.

7. Heat up a little butter in a frying pan or skillet.
    Place a golf ball–sized chunk of the mixture into
    the hot pan and flatten it with the spatula. Cook for
    a few minutes on each side until golden brown. If
    you are not sure, keep flipping it.

Note: *These pancakes can be served on their own, but they
are much nicer with a little of your favorite dip. Try them
with Fermented Pepper Hummus (page 90) or a large dollop of guacamole.*

Komugizuke

YIELD: N/A, as it is ongoing   PREP TIME: A few minutes a day, maybe for life
FERMENTATION TIME: Initially a few days, speeding up to a few hours

Nukazuke is a popular ferment in Japan. The word *nukazuke* roughly translates to mean rice bran pickles. Since rice bran is rather expensive and difficult to come by, I decided that a good American alternative would be komugizuke or wheat pickles.

As with sourdough bread, good komugizuke needs some daily attention. The attention is minimal in respect to the amount of time a day it needs you. However, it is critical that you run your hand

through the bran daily. Doing so not only aerates it, but helps feed it with fresh microbes from your hands. Avoid stirring your bran bed with soapy hands, as the soap will kill off the bacteria.

The stirring is imperative, and it is said that some of the really committed nukazuke *parents* travel with their nukazuke pot in order to keep up the regime. Likewise, making komugizuke really is for the dedicated fermenter. I am ashamed to admit that, even with my experience, the first time I tried this I made a grave mistake. By the third week I noticed that the bran really didn't smell great, in fact it smelled like something had died in it. The pickles also tasted a little more than funky, sour even. I had been away for a long weekend and left instructions to stir the bed every day; however, it got stirred only once. I'd also gotten a little worried that there wasn't enough moisture, and I'd added a little too much water before leaving.

If yours starts to smell like this, don't worry

too much. There is a fix that might work: Try stirring in a tablespoon of mustard powder and two cleaned and crushed eggshells. Try some pickles 24 hours later and take a whiff of the air around your komugizuke crock. If the smell is off and the pickles still taste sour, then repeat the process. If all is well, then continue with your "parenting regime" as instructed.

If it seems like a lot of effort, don't lose heart because the final result means that you can ferment your vegetables in hours rather than days. What's more, the resulting flavor is complex and fascinating—I'd wager unlike anything you have ever tasted before. The bran gives it a deep flavor that is lifted by the ginger, enhanced by the salt, and then injected with umami. All of this is followed by an aftertaste that combines them all, along with the beer or sake that originally went in.

continued

INGREDIENTS

One 5-inch (20-cm) square of kombu (seaweed), cut into 1-inch (3-cm) pieces

2 pounds (900 g) wheat bran (or rice bran if you can find it), more if needed

6 tablespoons (108 g) sea salt

2 cups (500 ml) ale-style, yet not heavily hopped, beer or sake (or 2 cups filtered or unchlorinated water and one slice of bread, crumbled up into crumbs)

1¼ cups (310 ml) filtered or unchlorinated water

3 outer leaves of cabbage

3 garlic cloves

2 raw carrots or 3½ ounces (100 g) radishes or any vegetables you have to spare other than onions, plus an additional 10½ ounces (300 g) vegetables to "feed" the bran bed

1 dried chili

1 inch fresh ginger

INSTRUCTIONS

Day 1

1. If using dried seaweed, rehydrate by pouring boiling water over it and leaving it for 30 minutes.

2. Meanwhile, lightly toast the bran over medium-low heat. Considering how lightweight bran is, you'll notice that 2 pounds is a large volume, and you'll need either a very large pan or you'll have to do this in batches. Either way, stir frequently to avoid overly browning or burning. I found it much easier to do in batches than piling it into a pan that wasn't quite big enough. You'll know when it is toasted enough as it will smell a bit like a bakery, and the bran will turn from a light shade of brown to a darker one. It should also be dry and powdery, 5 to 10 minutes or more depending on how big your batches are. This step, although not essential, adds an extra richness of flavor to the pickles.

3. Add the bran to a very large crock, at least 3 quarts (3 L) in volume, dump in the sea salt, and mix by hand.

4. Pour in the beer and give the bran bed another mix. If you don't wish to use any alcohol in your komugizuke, you can substitute for 2 cups water at this point with one bread slice worth of breadcrumbs. Top up with 1¼ cups water; if you rehydrated the seaweed, you can use some of that water. The bran bed should now be the consistency of wet sand (one poke of the finger will leave an indentation). It should also be free of any pockets of dry bran, so mix very thoroughly. For the sake of space you may wish to decrease the size of this recipe, or you may even increase it. If you do, remember that you need roughly 13 percent of salt by weight of the bran. And the water- or liquid-to-bran ratio is 1:1 by weight. So if using 1 pound (500 g) of bran, you'll need to use 1 pound (15 fl oz; 500 ml) of water.

5. Add the cabbage leaves, garlic, carrots or vegetables, chilli, and ginger. Be sure they are completely covered by the bran and that they are not touching

each other. Pat down the bran bed and put a plate over the top of it, weigh it down, and cover it.

Day 2

1. Stir the bran bed by hand ensuring that the plate is placed over the bran after stirring. The water should have risen above the plate. If it hasn't, then add some more brine at the rate of 1 tablespoon sea salt per 1 cup (250 ml) water. If the opposite is true, and there is too much water, rising by 1 inch or more, then skim off. The stirring is very important, as it helps prevent mold forming in the bran.

Day 3

1. Repeat instructions from day 2.

Day 4

1. Take out the vegetables, cut them up, and eat them if you wish or compost them.

2. Add another 3½ ounces (100 g) of vegetables. What you are doing during this first two weeks is getting the culture started—don't forget you'll be rewarded with delicious tasting vegetables that pickle/ferment really quickly!

3. Test your bran bed and top up with brine if required at a rate of 1 tablespoon sea salt per cup (250 ml) of water.

Day 5

1. Just as before, stir the bran bed by hand ensuring that you weigh the bran down with the plate again. The water should have risen above the plate. If it hasn't, then add some more brine at the rate of 1 tablespoon sea salt per 1 cup (250 ml) water. If the opposite is true, and there is too much water, rising by 1 inch or more, then skim off.

Day 6

1. Repeat instructions from day 5.

Day 7

1. Repeat instructions from day 5.

continued

Day 8

1. Take out the vegetables and taste them. They should be starting to get sour by now. Add another 3½ ounces (100 g) of vegetables.

2. Depending on how much bran has been sticking to your vegetables, you may need to add some more bran to top up the bran bed so that it is as full as it was in the beginning. If so, toast it as before, add it to the bran bed, and ensure you add enough brine mix (1 cup water: 1 tablespoon salt). The first time I tried this recipe, this was the point I started to notice that the bran really didn't smell great. If this is the case, then you might need to rectify it. I had added too much liquid and it hadn't been stirred every day, which harbored the wrong types of bacteria. But don't be too alarmed, as you can add more toasted bran and keep stirring. Hopefully the smell will go away and you will be okay. Or you might have to start again. But try not to be too overly cautious, as there will be some pretty funky smells emanating from your crock. If you have stirred daily, it isn't too overly moist, and the smell isn't totally overpowering, then you are good to go.

Day 9

1. Repeat instructions from day 5.

Day 10

1. Repeat instructions from day 5, ensuring there is enough moisture in the bran bed.

Day 11

1. Repeat instructions from day 8.

Day 12

1. Repeat instructions from day 5, ensuring there is enough moisture in the bran bed.

Day 13

1. Your bran bed should now be fully up to speed and teeming with life. Keep stirring daily and adding vegetables. Smaller vegetables can be cultured in a few hours and larger ones overnight. Ferment cucumbers, any kind of radish, carrots, broccoli, or whatever takes your fancy—just steer clear of potatoes and onions, which are not edible using this method.

Day 14 and beyond

1. Once your bran bed is up and running, it will still need a bit of tender loving care. I have to admit I forget to turn mine every single day and manage around once every 1½ days on average, and that does the job. I also ensure that it stays moist, keep it covered, and occasionally add more bran. I am rewarded with very quickly fermented vegetables whenever I need them.

Sourdough Starter and Bread

YIELD: 1 starter SUGGESTED JAR SIZES: 8 ounce (250 ml), 1 pint (500 ml), 1 quart (1 L), 2 quart (2 L)
PREP TIME: 7 days FERMENTATION TIME: 7 days

Sourdough bread, believe it or not, is bread made from dough that tastes sour—who'd have guessed! It is made by creating a yeast culture that helps the bread to rise. There is something quite special about making bread from the yeast that are flying around your kitchen. It somehow feels like part of your home is in the bread!

I recommend making some bread, then adding your own cheese (Fresh Curd Cheese, page 248), butter (Fermented Butter, page 256), ham, a few slices of fermented tomato (Ukrainian Fermented Tomatoes, page 128), and a pickled cuke (Fermented Dilly "Cukes," page 132) for the ultimate in fermented sandwiches. The result will be the envy of the lunch break.

INGREDIENTS

4 tablespoons (50 g) flour*
4 tablespoons (50 ml) filtered or unchlorinated water*

* One thing to bear in mind when making a sourdough starter is that you always add the same amount of flour and water to the same amount of sourdough starter.

INSTRUCTIONS

Day 1

1. Put the flour and water into an 8-ounce (250-ml) jar and mix well. Leave for around 12 hours, placing a square of material over the top to keep out any insects.

Day 2

1. Transfer to a larger 1-pint (16-oz; 500-ml) jar. Add 4 tablespoons (50 g) flour and 4 tablespoons (50 ml) water to the jar and mix well.

continued

Day 3

1. Discard half the starter. Add 4 tablespoons (50 g) flour and 4 tablespoons (50 ml) water to the jar and mix well.

Day 4

1. You should hopefully now be seeing some bubbles. Don't worry too much if not, but there could be a chance that you are in a yeast desert—in which case, you may want to move your starter to your car or to a friend's house to get it going.

    Transfer the starter to a 1-quart (1-L) jar. Add 8 tablespoons (100 g) flour and 8 tablespoons (100 ml) water to the jar and mix thoroughly.

Day 5

1. You should most certainly have some bubbles now; if not, then you need to take action as it might not be working. Did you use soap at any point? Are you in a yeast desert? Try increasing the feeding regime by increasing the size of your starter every 12 hours instead of every day. Check the temperature too; is it too cold at night perhaps? Ideally, it should be kept in the range of 70 to 80°F (21 to 27C°).

    Transfer the contents of the 1-quart jar to a larger 2-quart (2-L) jar. Add 1 cup (200 g) flour and 1 cup (250 ml) water and mix thoroughly.

    Cover and leave to continue its life cycle.

Day 6

1. Your starter should be alive and thriving at this point, and it is very nearly ready. Discard half of the starter. If this seems like a waste after such an amount of time, you could try and offer it to a friend, neighbor, or an interesting-looking person on the bus.

    Add in 1 cup (200 g) flour and 1 cup (250 ml) water and stir thoroughly. Cover and leave it to ferment for another day.

Day 7

1. Your starter is now ready to use. Don't forget to save 8 ounces (230 g) when you first use it. You can then follow from day 1 and keep the process going. See below for how to maintain your starter.

MAINTAINING YOUR SOURDOUGH STARTER

A well-maintained sourdough starter can outlive its baker. I have heard of sourdough starters that are over a century old, even older. Of course, you don't have to commit to keeping yours alive for this long, but in order to have it on hand whenever you feel like baking a loaf, you will need to feed it regularly. Your goal then is to keep the active bacteria and yeast healthy.

Feed it just like you did throughout the process of starting your starter, and remember that you always want to double up each time. So, unless you want your starter to get really big, you'll be discarding throughout the process. In reality this means adding 1 cup of flour and 1 cup of water to every 2 cups of starter, then discarding half the starter the next day before adding another cup of flour and cup of water.

If you are not making a ton of bread, you can store your starter in the refrigerator. The recommendation is for around two weeks, but I have successfully used a two-month-old starter that I found hidden behind many fermentation jars in the back of my refrigerator. In this case, I revived it over three days by following a daily feeding process of the kind I just outlined. The resulting loaf was delicious.

Baking a Sourdough Loaf

YIELD: 1 loaf
PREP TIME: 30 minutes
RISING TIME: 10 to 15 hours to rise twice
BAKING TIME: 30 minutes

Now that you have your sourdough, you'll want to get baking with it. You can use it to make pizza dough or scones, but I recommend at least trying to bake a loaf of bread first. This will help you get used to working with it before you go off experimenting. This following recipe is for a simple white sourdough loaf.

I should point out that the sourdough starter can be quite sticky and hard to weigh—you have been warned!

INGREDIENTS

4 cups (1 lb; 500 g) strong white flour
12 ounces (340 g) starter
2 teaspoons sea salt
1 cup (250 ml) tepid filtered or unchlorinated water
Olive oil

INSTRUCTIONS

1. Mix the flour, starter, and salt in a large mixing bowl, then start gradually adding the tepid water bit by bit. Keep mixing with your hands until you have a soft, and not sticky, dough that has taken in all the flour from the bowl. There is a good chance you won't need all the water.

2. Brush your chopping board or countertop with olive oil.

3. Transfer the dough to your chopping board and knead for 10 minutes or so until the dough has formed a soft skin and feels smooth and silky.

4. Clean, then thoroughly dry your mixing bowl and coat with olive oil. Plop in the dough and cover with a tea towel. The cleaning also helps to warm up a cold metal or glass bowl, which can affect the dough, especially during the winter months.

5. Leave to rise for around five hours at 70 to 76°F (21 to 24°C). In this time, the bread should double in size. If it hasn't, then leave it for a little longer.

6. Punch the dough in the middle to knock all the air out. Roll it back into a ball and lightly dust with flour.

7. If you have a proofing basket, or even a banneton, put the dough into it. If you don't have one, then line a bowl with a tea towel and pop the dough in that instead. The dough takes on the shape and characteristics of what you put it in at this stage, and this is how you get the classic sourdough-looking bread. It is mostly cosmetic, and so a bowl and tea towel will save you the expense.

8. Dust your loaf with flour and proof for an additional 5 to 10 hours, again at 70 to 76°F (21 to 24°C). Don't let it get all wrinkly, as this means it has overproofed, which is more likely at the warmer end of the temperature scale.

9. Preheat your oven to 400°F (200°C) and put a baking tray half filled with water in the bottom of the oven.

10. Line another baking tray with parchment paper and gently pop the loaf onto the baking tray once it has finished proofing. Slash the top with a razor or sharp knife.

11. Bake for 30 minutes or until it is golden brown and has a hollow sound when you tap it. If you are unsure of what a hollow sound sounds like, think more of a drum that echoes inside the bread than a thud. The bread will kind of wobble in your hand if it isn't ready. If that is the case, pop it back in for another five minutes before testing again. Allow to cool on a wire rack, and then perhaps serve it with Fermented Butter (see page 256).

Sourdough Pizza Base

YIELD: Five 12-inch pizza bases   PREP TIME: 5 hours (plus overnight if doing a slow rise)
FERMENTATION TIME: 12 hours (30 minutes if using the quick method)

Unfortunately, most of us don't have the time to make a sourdough loaf every day, and there is a real chance that you'll make the starter, use it for a week, then forget about those poor millions of microbes. Therefore, it is worth having a few other recipes up your sleeve for your starter—step up sourdough pizza! It's a delicious and healthy alternative to store-bought pizza and quicker than making bread every day!

Many recipes for sourdough pizza dough take a day or even two to make. This one has been designed for convenience. It can be started when you get in from work or school, ready for your evening meal.

INGREDIENTS

4 cups (500 g) white bread flour

1¼ cups (300 ml) Sourdough Starter (page 169)

1 cup (250 ml) room-temperature filtered or unchlorinated water

Large pinch of salt

INSTRUCTIONS

1. Put all the ingredients into your mixing bowl and mix well.

2. Once you have a rough dough, knead it for about 10 minutes before returning it to the mixing bowl and covering with a tea towel. Leave in a warm place for at least 30 minutes.

   It is at this point that you could leave it for four hours at room temperature and then overnight in the refrigerator. If you have time, you should try this method at least once. It does make for a better pizza. However, 30 minutes will suffice.

3. Divide the dough into five sections. You can freeze some if five pizzas are too many.

4. On a floured surface, roll your five sections to 12-inch pizza bases. Grease your baking trays and put the bases onto them. Cover them with a tea towel and leave them to rise a bit more: 10 minutes if you are really short on time or 1 hour for that more leisurely weekend pizza—you can even wait another day if you wish and go for a slow rise in the refrigerator.

5. Preheat the oven to 500°F (260°C).

6. Add the toppings of your choice to your pizzas.

7. Pop into your oven and bake for seven to eight minutes, or until it is really hot right in the middle.

Akamu/Pap/Ogi from Popcorn Kernels

YIELD: 1 cup (120 to 150 g) of fine powder
PREP TIME: 4 hours plus   FERMENTATION TIME: 3 to 5 days

Akamu, also known as pap or ogi, is a kind of Nigerian corn porridge; it's well known as a food that is fed to growing children and is loved by adults too. It's quite a process to make it, but I think it offers quite an insight into a food culture that is often overlooked. It takes a while to master the art of making ogi/pap, so don't worry if your first efforts yield much less than you had hoped.

Ogi/pap is rather bland and tasteless, but its flavor is lifted when some sugar is stirred in. The tang of the ferment isn't as strong as in many vegetable ferments, but the fermentation does add a depth of flavor. It is certainly more appetizing than ogi/pap made with straight unfermented cornmeal. Having blind-tasted fermented and unfermented ogi/pap side by side, I can say that I intuitively seek out the fermented cornmeal version. This could be due to the presence of *Lactobacillus plantarum*, a strain of lactobacillus that some studies suggest can help with a host of health issues including anxiety and eczema.

Traditionally, sweetened condensed milk is added to taste, although I prefer a teaspoon of brown sugar along with a big pinch of garam masala or Chinese five spice.

INGREDIENTS

18 ounces (500 g) popcorn kernels
Filtered or unchlorinated water
More water
... more water still

INSTRUCTIONS

Days 1 and 2

1. Pour the popcorn kernels into a large bowl or crock, submerse with water, then cover loosely with a tea towel.

2. Leave in a warm place until day 3.

Days 3 and 4

1. Boil and cool more water and swap out the original water. Leave until day 5.

Day 5

1. Look at the kernels. They should have expanded up to twice the size and will be soft when you bite into one. There will also be some bubbles on the surface of the water, and it will have a bit of a funky smell. Now the real work begins.

2. Drain the water off and rinse the corn well.

3. Add 1 cup at a time to your food processor and cover with water. Blend until it is a smooth paste and continue until you have ground all the corn.

4. Pass the corn through a sieve and keep the water. This, too, is better to do in small batches. Keep squeezing the corn as you go. At this stage you are trying to separate the chaff—the coarse, thicker bits of corn. When you think you have squeezed out as much as possible, have another squeeze. The first time I made this I didn't get anything like a maximum yield, so don't worry if you find the

same, it takes practice. The trick is to be slow and steady.

5. Once you have passed the corn through a sieve, discard the thick yellow chaff; this is the

continued

177

fragmentary remains of the outer shell and you are trying to keep a hold of the good stuff on the inside. The chaff is traditionally fed to livestock, so if you or a neighbor keep livestock, you can do the same. If not then perhaps try feeding it to a pet dog. Those living in a city apartment without pets could feed some to the squirrels in the park or compost it.

6. You will now be left with some liquid that is still full of some solid matter; this is the corn becoming your ogi. Pass the liquid through a fine piece of cheesecloth. You will want to pass the pap through two increasingly finer weaves of cheesecloth as this helps to filter it.

7. On the final squeeze, allow the pap to drip down, then tie the cloth in knots until you have squeezed out the last bit of liquid.

8. Place the ogi-filled cheesecloth in a wide bowl and then put something heavy, like a couple of thick books or some house bricks or stones wrapped up in a fabric bag, on it. Whatever you choose, it needs to fit neatly into the bowl so that all its weight is pressing down on the cheesecloth. This will help to squeeze out the very last bit of liquid and will leave you with your pap ready to use.

9. To make the porridge, add about ½ cup of pap to a bowl and slowly add up to 1 cup (250 ml) of near boiling water—less if you want a thicker porridge. Keep stirring. It should start to thicken.

Rice Flour Idlis

YIELD: 20 idlis

PREP TIME: 1 hour, (plus 24 hours soaking time)   FERMENTATION TIME: 8 to 12 hours

Travel to India and you'll see idlis served as breakfast all over the place. Variations have traveled into Sri Lanka, too, with ingredients being switched out to suit local availability. Perhaps the most well-known variation is rava idli (wheat idli).

There are recipes out there for idlis made without fermentation, but I think the acidity and texture of a good traditional idli comes from the fermentation process.

You may have some trouble sourcing the urid dhal. Just know that these beans can go by many different names: lentils, split black matpe bean, kaali dal, split black gram, vigna mungo, urad bean, urid bean, minapa pappu, and mungo bean. If you can't find them at your local world food supermarket, then try searching online for matpe beans. It may also be difficult to get a hold of the traditional rice to make this recipe, so

continued

to remove that headache I use rice flour. If you can't get a hold of fenugreek seeds, you can use black or yellow mustard seeds instead.

In addition to the ingredients to make idlis, you will need special idli molds. Because this is an Indian staple food, you might be able to put a request out across any of your social networks for these molds. Otherwise, you should be able to find the molds online through the bigger retailers or at world food supermarkets. I have used 1½-inch (5-cm) ramekins in the past, and if you do the same then you will need to add a little more batter. As a result, the recipe will make fewer idlis, but it just about works and the idlis come out like little rice muffins.

You will also need to know how to steam them. I use a pressure cooker and use it with the weight/whistle turned off/open so the idlis are steamed, not pressure cooked.

These days you can buy electric steamers and pressure cookers that will also cook rice, make yogurt, and slow cook. I recommend getting one, because it uses less energy than a stove and will eventually pay for itself in fuel costs.

INGREDIENTS

1 cup (8 oz; 220 g) urid dhal

3 cups (750 ml) room-temperature filtered or unchlorinated water, divided

½ cup (4 oz; 100 g) rice flour

1 teaspoon fenugreek seeds

1 teaspoon sea salt

Butter or oil for greasing

INSTRUCTIONS

1. Place the urid dhal in a bowl and pour over 2 cups of the water and leave overnight. The lentils will expand to at least twice their original size, absorbing much of the water. Using room-temperature water will aid with absorption as the warmer the water, the quicker the lentils will take it up.

2. Drain off any of the remaining water into a separate bowl and retain, as this can be used again for processing. Add the soaked urid dhal to the food processor and mix until they start to look like hummus. You can add some of the water back if you need to; you may even need more filtered water.

3. In a separate bowl, mix the rice flour, fenugreek seeds, and salt and keep adding the remaining 1 cup water until it makes a thick batter that you can pour.

4. Mix both batters together and leave in a warm place for 8 to 12 hours. After this time the batter should have risen to around twice its original size, and it should be bubbling too.

5. Grease up to 20 idli molds and pour or spoon in your mixture one by one. Don't fill right to the very top but don't be sparing either; 80 to 90 percent full is a good guide.

6. Place the idli molds into your steamer and set for 10 minutes—if using a pressure cooker ensure that the whistle/steam valve is open.

7. Check after 10 minutes; they should be done. If they are flat instead of firm, or fluffy and looking like mini flying saucers, then you will need to give them an additional five minutes.

8. They are best served with Coconut Chutney; see page 100.

Rice Flour Dosas

YIELD: 4 small dosas   PREP TIME: 30 minutes (plus 24 hours soaking time)
FERMENTATION TIME: 8 to 12 hours

The keen eyed amongst you will notice that this dosa recipe uses the same ingredients as Rice Flour Idlis (page 179), plus a few extras and without the need for a pressure cooker!

I stopped eating regular pancakes a while ago, but I continue to eat these little rice flour pancakes. They are deliciously crisp, tasty, and offer a great alternative for anyone with a wheat intolerance. What's more, they contain more digestible fiber than wheat pancakes and are better for you, too, so perhaps they could become your alternative to regular breakfast pancakes. I like mine plain with nothing on them at all. Traditionally, they are served with coconut chutney, leftover lentils, or last night's curry.

You will see that I've added lovage for an alternate ingredient, which is in no way authentic. However, I have found dosas to be immensely adaptable, so go ahead and add your own favorite herbs and spices.

INGREDIENTS

8 ounces (220 g) urid dhal

3 cups (750 ml) room-temperature filtered or unchlorinated water, divided

½ cup (100 g) rice flour

1 teaspoon fenugreek seeds

1 teaspoon sea salt

1 inch (2.5 cm) fresh ginger

1 ounce (30 g) fresh parsley or cilantro or lovage

1 tablespoon butter or oil for frying

INSTRUCTIONS

1. Place the urid dhal in a bowl and pour over 2 cups of the water. Leave overnight and the lentils will expand to at least twice their original size, absorbing much of the water. Using room-temperature water will aid with absorption, as the warmer the water, the quicker the lentils will take it up.

2. Drain off any of the remaining water into a separate bowl and retain, as this can be used again for processing. Add the soaked urid dhal to the food processor and mix until they start to look like hummus. You can add some of the water back if you need to; you may even need more filtered water.

3. Mix the rice flour, fenugreek seeds, and salt and keep adding the remaining 1 cup water until it makes a thick batter that you can pour.

4. Mix both batters together and leave in a warm place for 8 to 12 hours. After this time the batter should have risen to around twice its original size, and it should be bubbling too. If neither have happened, then leave for an additional 8 hours.

5. Grate the ginger and chop the fresh herbs. Mix them into your batter along with enough water to turn the batter into a thinner consistency, similar to regular pancake batter.

6. Meanwhile, heat 1 tablespoon of butter or oil over high heat in your frying pan or griddle until it starts to bubble; be careful not to scorch the butter. Reduce the heat a little and pour in your batter, ensuring they are as thin as you can get them without being full of holes. Don't worry if your first batch sticks to the pan and then takes a whole load of effort to scrape off; this is a learning curve. The trick to cooking any kind of pancake is being sure there is even heat across all of the pan, as it's the uneven heat that makes them stick!

7. After just a few minutes of cooking the dosas will start to thicken on the top, flip them over and cook on the other side. You are hoping to get both sides golden brown.

Boza

YIELD: 6 pints (3 L) boza   SUGGESTED FERMENTATION VESSEL: Crock
PREP TIME: 1 to 3 hours (plus 8 hours soaking time)   FERMENTATION TIME: 3 days

Boza is a drink, pictured on page 160, which is popular around the stunningly beautiful and mountainous Caucasus region. To give you a quick geography lesson, this region is located on the border of Eastern Europe and Western Asia between the Black Sea and the Caspian Sea.

There are a few regional variations across the Caucasus, and there has been much debate on what makes for "real boza." Some recipes call for rice, some for proso millet (also known as red millet). The other contentious ingredient is of course the yeast—is it proper boza without authentic boza yeast? A 1997 study published in the *International Journal of Food Microbiology* found that boza contained two types of yeast: *Saccharomyces uvarum* (83 percent) and *S. cerevisiae* (17 percent). There were also various strains of lactic acid bacteria.

As I didn't have a boza starter to faithfully re-create the traditional recipe, I decided to improvise the best I could. I mixed my sauerkraut starter culture with two strains of store-bought yeast (a red wine strain and an ale strain, *Saccharomyces uvarum*). I then compared this with some boza I'd made using just one yeast strain, as many recipes suggest; I am pleased to say that, in this author's opinion, the attention to detail was worth it. The two-yeast and sauerkraut starter culture boza was far more complex and ultimately, delicious!

INGREDIENTS

2 cups bulgur wheat

14 cups (3½ L) cold filtered or unchlorinated water, divided

2½ teaspoons (5 g) powdered red wine yeast

½ teaspoon (1 g) Nottingham ale yeast

3 cups granulated sugar, divided

1 tablespoon starter culture (from yogurt or sauerkraut) or boza starter culture (optional)

INSTRUCTIONS

1. Scatter the bulgur wheat across the bottom of a nonmetallic crockpot and pour over 10 cups of the water.

2. Leave for at least eight hours in a warm spot so that the bulgur wheat absorbs as much of the liquid as possible.

3. Place the pot on your stovetop and gently simmer until soft—this should take between 45 minutes and 2 hours. During this time stir about eight times; this will ensure that all the grains are cooked evenly and that none stick to the bottom of the pan.

4. At this stage you may wish to activate your yeasts and to take your starter culture out of the fridge. To activate the yeasts, place in small separate bowls, add 2 tablespoons of warm water and ½ teaspoon of sugar to each, and leave in a warm place. I use separate bowls so I can ensure that both yeasts are activated.

5. Take the bulgur wheat off the heat, add 4 cups of the cold water, and blend until smooth.

6. Next, pass it through a sieve; you may need to ease the process by agitating it through with a spoon. (Traditionally, these leftover larger particles, which are left in the sieve, are used in baking. I used them with an egg and some milk to make a sort of pancake.)

7. Check the temperature and ensure it has cooled to 70 to 72°F (about 21°C) before stirring in the yeast and the starter culture. If you add the yeast at too high a temperature, you will overwork it and may get some off flavors.

8. Leave for 3 days at a warmish room temperature—above 69°F and below 75°F (20 to 24°C). Within half a day, a lovely mat of yeast should be starting to cover your brew. If it doesn't, you may have added dead yeast, so try adding some from a different packet or batch.

9. Return now and again to give your mixture a stir.

10. After three days your boza is ready. I like it as is but you can add flavorings; traditionally this might be vanilla extract, or you could try some grated nutmeg. Mix in a little water to thin out the drink and then refrigerate before serving. Drink within two weeks.

Note: *After experimenting with yeast on its own and yeast with sauerkraut starter culture to make boza, I can confirm that there is a difference between the two. The boza made with yeast and sauerkraut starter culture has more of a tang and has greater body too. In my opinion it is far superior, and I strongly suggest you include starter culture in your recipe. Enjoy your boza!*

Kvass

YIELD: 10 quarts (10 L) kvass

PREP TIME: 13 hours   MINIMUM FERMENTATION TIME: 2 to 3 days

Whereas beet kvass is made with beets (see Beet Kvass, page 152), traditional kvass is made with rye bread. Despite its slight alcohol content (less than 2 percent ABV), kvass is given to children across much of Russia by well-meaning parents.

The word *kvass* is derived from the Proto-Slavic word that means "fermented drink." This rye bread or black bread version has been a common drink across Eastern Europe since before the Middle Ages.

It is thought of as more than just a drink among the rural poor of Eastern Europe, and it is often used as the basis for many stocks, soups, and broths. As the influence of Western culture, and our soft drinks, continues to permeate the region, so kvass is falling out of popularity. Ironically, Western culture is now starting to embrace fermented drinks, so there is a possibility that the big drink brands will start to sell kvass back to the Eastern Europeans.

I am not sure where this recipe came from originally, but it is the one I have been following for a few years now and it works well. I find the resulting drink is a little like beer and a little like a cola—although much deeper in flavor.

INGREDIENTS

10 quarts (10 L) filtered or unchlorinated water

1 small rye sourdough loaf

1 handful pomegranate seeds (optional)

10 dried figs

2.2 pounds (1 kg) sugar

1 teaspoon crushed coriander seeds

1 tablespoon Sourdough Starter (page 169)

One ½-ounce (15-g) packet dried ale yeast (Fermentis Safbrew T-58, for example; specialist yeasts such as this can be found at your local homebrew shop or specialist online stores)

INSTRUCTIONS

1. Bring the water to a boil in a large saucepan. Meanwhile, cut the rye bread into slices and toast. The toast might seem a little bit of an odd thing to add to a drink, but this helps to give the kvass a darker color and adds some flavor.

2. Remove the water from the heat and add the fruit, sugar, coriander seeds, and toast. Cover and leave for 12 hours to infuse and cool down.

3. Remove the toast and add the yeast.

4. Leave for at least two to three days at 59 to 75°F (15 to 24°C) to ferment, and aim to keep this temperature as stable as possible. If you can't, don't worry too much, as kvass is much more forgiving than beer.

5. Traditionally, kvass is bottled after two or three days fermenting in order for it to stay fizzy. If you decide to bottle after this time, I recommend placing it in the refrigerator and taking out the bottles every now and then to let out some air. I also recommend using strong flip-top bottles or plastic bottles if you take this option. It is best drunk within a few days but will keep for a few months.

Note: I tend to let kvass ferment for a little longer than what's required and to give it a bit of time in another fermentation vessel, just as I might when brewing beer (see A Simple Beer from Malt Extract on page 190). This involves siphoning the kvass out of the vessel it is in and pouring it into another vessel. This second vessel needs an airlock because the kvass is still fermenting, though at a much slower rate.

It's not that I think doing this adds a huge amount to the flavor, as it does with beer, but it does cut down accidents, because the kvass becomes less volatile. The downside is that the final product can be less fizzy. When bottling, do not use beer bottles with crown caps, even after taking this optional step, as the kvass can still be a touch unstable.

BREWING BEER

There are two beers you will always remember, the first one you drink and the first one you brew. I didn't really like the taste of either, but it didn't stop me from falling in love with beer and wanting to persevere. Thankfully, I did continue and I have since won awards for my brewing.

The problem with my first-ever brewed beer was that I pitched (added) the yeast when the wort (the unfermented mixture of hops, water, and malted barley) was over 80°F (26°C), which is way too hot. It should have been closer to 68°F (20°C). In this single example I have not only explained a fundamental and frequent error made by rookie homebrewers, but you have learned pretty much the basics of making a beer. That is how easy it can be!

By far the easiest way to make a beer for the first time is to use a kit. I won't explain how to make a kit beer in these pages, as it is unlikely that you'll buy one that doesn't come with simple instructions. If not, a quick online search will yield a world of tutorials. It's easy to find a YouTuber who has filmed the whole process.

The next stage up from making beer from a kit is to make an extract brew—that is to say, making beer using malt extract. This is a great way to go because by using a malt extract the hard work of extracting the sugars from the grain has already been done for you. I go into more detail on this process in the recipe for making beer (see A Simple Beer from Malt Extract on page 190). Finally, you can make a full-grain beer: This process involves "mashing," which means converting grain starches to fermentable sugars by keeping them in water at 140 to 158°F (60 to 71°C) for a set time.

You will need a bit of gear too. You can buy kits online or from your local homebrew shop. I highly recommend seeking out and buying from your local homebrew shop, as doing so not only helps support a local tax-paying business and therefore your local economy, but it will also (most likely) come with some pretty sound advice—even if you don't ask for it!

CHOOSING INGREDIENTS FOR BEER

Beer can be altered completely depending on which ingredients you put in it. There are worlds of difference among an East Coast IPA, a UK porter, a Belgium saison, or a domestic lager. When brewing at home you are in charge of these ingredients and you can alter them as you wish. There is already a *Brewing Everything* book in The Countryman Press Know-How series, and I highly recommend reading it, along with my *The Perfect Pint* if you are inspired to make more beer after trying out the beer recipes in this book.

Malt extract varies from very light to very dark. The darker extracts will give you some of the flavors of darker beers, but really you want to add steeped grains to add a more robust flavor. There is also dry malt extract and liquid malt extract—I prefer to use liquid, as this is what I used when I first started brewing. If you use a dry malt extract, then you will need to use 84 percent the amount of dried malt extract in a recipe as you would liquid—so for a 7-pound (3-kg) recipe, you'll need 5 pounds 14 ounces (2.8 kg).

Wild hops can be very interesting to play around with. I highly recommend you try to find some and then use them "green." That is to say you should use twice as much as a recipe says and use them fresh. I suggest you choose hops by their flavor profile. Start reading the side of beer bottles to get an idea of the different hops out there. One of the key ways to choose a hop is to look at its bitterness, which is measured by alpha acids, often marked as AA. The higher the alpha acids, the more bitter the hop.

If using grains, it would be wise to get yourself acquainted with the different types. There are base, roasted, and specialty. The base makes up between 60 and 100 percent of grains used. Roasted and specialty grains add color and flavor. The total amount of grains used in a beer is what's known as the "grain bill."

Last, there is yeast. This can really alter the flavor of a beer. A lager, ale, and saison could all start with exactly the same ingredients, but obtain much of their distinctive characteristics from the yeast. The key is to match the yeast to what you are making (at first, at least). Simply use an ale yeast for an ale, a lager yeast for a lager, and so forth. Some yeasts are easier to work with than others, and you'll get to know what each yeast likes over time. But mostly, if you can keep the temperature pretty constant and within the range that the yeast likes, then you'll be fine.

A Simple Beer from Malt Extract

YIELD: 5 gallons (19 L) beer

PREP TIME: 2 hours   MINIMUM FERMENTATION TIME: 2 weeks

This recipe can be made using other ingredients other than just hops. I once taught a group of people how to make this beer and they went off and made their own versions using what they could find—lovage (tasty), ramps (terrible), carrot tops (terrible), and chamomile flowers (interesting). The rule of thumb about making herbal beers is to think about it critically: Have you ever tried any alcoholic drink that tastes of garlic or carrot tops? Beyond taste, also make sure you are not using anything poisonous!

INGREDIENTS

6 gallons (22 L) filtered or unchlorinated water, divided

7 pounds (3 kg) liquid (amber) malt extract

1 ounce bittering hops (hops with 7 AA or more, Haller-tauer Magnum, for example)

One 1/3-ounce (11 g) packet dry ale yeast (Safale US-04 or Danstar Nottingham, for example)

2 ounces aroma hops (hops with less than 7 AA, Cascade, for example)

3 ounces (85 g) sugar or 4½ ounces (130 g) dried malt extract

INSTRUCTIONS

1. Sterilize everything that will touch the wort/beer.

2. If you have a wort chiller, you can boil the full 6 gallons of water and then add the malt extract and stir thoroughly. Once you can't feel any gloopiness as you stir, it's time to add the bittering hops. If you don't have a wort chiller, bring 3 gallons of water to a boil and then add the malt extract and

stir thoroughly. You'll notice that there is an extra gallon of water in the recipe than in the final yield; this is because you will lose roughly 1 gallon in the boiling process.

4. Rehydrate the yeast as per package instructions.

5. Boil, but not over vigorously, for the next 50 minutes and then add 1 ounce of the aroma hops. At the 55-minute mark, add the last 1 ounce of aroma hops.

6. Boil for an additional five minutes. Then very carefully strain through a muslin cloth into a large fermentation vessel. The aim is to get rid of any hop debris.

7. If you don't have a wort chiller, top up your fermentation vessel with enough cold water to bring the total volume up to 5 gallons (19 L). If you do have a wort chiller, it is time to use it! Take a temperature reading; you will need to get the temperature down to about 68°F (18°C). Also take a hydrometer reading, which should read 1.050, or as close as possible.

8. Pitch (add) the yeast.

9. Put the lid on your fermentation vessel and add water or, better still, whisky to the airlock, unless you have one without an airlock—in which case, loosely cover it. Leave in a space that keeps a constant temperature of between 60 and 70°F (15 and 21°C).

10. Check that it is bubbling—if it doesn't after 3 days, then repitch some yeast or move it to a warmer spot.

11. After a week take a hydrometer reading. Hopefully, that should read in the region of 1.010 or lower, depending on which yeast you opted for. If it is higher, try moving it to a warmer spot or pitch some more yeast.

12. Bring ½ cup (125 ml) water to a boil and stir in the sugar. Allow to cool. Add this to your beer and stir in with a sterilized spoon. Be gentle, you don't want to disturb the sediment.

13. Have a beer (optional but advised).

14. Siphon into bottles or a keg. If using bottles, then don't forget to leave a little headroom. A quick heads-up: I sometimes find this part of the job a little tedious and recommend doing it with a friend or putting on the radio.

15. Leave the bottles for at least another week, if not two. A beer this strength will keep for at least six months—although I have drunk one that was two years old and it was still pretty good!

A Simple All-Grain Beer

YIELD: 5 gallons (19 L) beer
PREP TIME: 5 to 12 hours   MINIMUM FERMENTATION TIME: 2 weeks

Your own homebrewed beer can be as good or even better than a lot of the commercial beers out there. Indeed, many brewers test out a recipe at home before brewing it commercially.

I understand that making your first beer may seem like a daunting process, but in truth it is relatively straightforward. As brewing archaeologist (yes, there are brewing archaeologists) Merryn Dineley puts it, "Making ale from the grain is a process that has not changed across the millennia. You take the crushed grain, you heat it with water to make a sweet mash. Next, lauter and sparge (this means rinse the grains) to extract a clear wort (unfermented beer), then boil it up with herbs."

Like learning to cook, making sauerkraut, or baking bread, making beer just takes practice.

In addition, beer making has its own terminology that can be hard to follow. So before getting into all that terminology, I'd like to give you the steps for making beer in plain English:

1. Crush grains.
2. Make a kind of porridge with the grains and water and leave at 148 to 158°F (60 to 71°C) for approximately one hour .
3. Drain off the liquid.
4. Rinse the grains and drain off that liquid too.
5. Boil it with herbs/hops.
6. Ferment.

It really is that simple.

INGREDIENTS

20½ quarts (20 L) filtered or unchlorinated water, divided, plus an additional 5 quarts (5 L) boiling water for warming up your mash tun

9 pounds (4 kg) pale malt

2 pounds 3 ounces (1 kg) wheat malt

9 ounces (250 g) Crystal 40L malt

1 ounce bittering hops (hops with 7 AA or more, Haller-tauer Magnum, for example)

2 ounces aroma hops (hops with less than 7 AA, Cascade, for example)

One 1/3-ounce (11 g) packet Wyeast 1056 American ale (dried) yeast

3 ounces (85 g) sugar or 4.5 ounces (130 g) dried malt extract, for priming

INSTRUCTIONS

1. Sterilize everything that will touch the wort/beer.

2. Bring 9½ quarts (9 L) of the water up to 167°F (75°C).

3. Swirl the additional 5 quarts of boiling water in a mash tun to warm it up. Then discard this water.

4. Add some of your malts to the mash tun and stir in the boiling water from step 2. Keep adding the three grains and the water bit by bit, stirring as it enters the mash tun, ensuring that all the grain is moistened and there are not pockets of air with dry grains in them.

5. Take a temperature reading: Is it around 154°F (68°C)? If hotter, allow to cool; but if cooler, then add a little more hot water.

6. Seal the mash tun and leave for 90 minutes. Check that the temperature inside doesn't drop below 149°F (65°C). If it does, add a little more hot water.

7. Start heating another 11 quarts (11 L) of the water to 171°F (77°C); this is your sparge water—the water that will rinse the grains.

8. Slowly turn the tap on your mash tun and allow to drain into your boiler/copper/brew pot.

9. Turn off tap and slowly add some of the sparge water over the grains. Ensure that all the grains come into contact with this water.

10. Put the lid back on the mash tun and leave for 10 minutes.

11. Drain, slowly adding more of the sparge water.

12. Take a note of the volume of the water. You may need to add a little more sparge water to bring this up to just above 5 gallons (19 L).

13. Now it's time for the boil. Turn on your boiler and start boiling. When boiling is reached, add the bittering hops and time another 55 minutes.

14. Add the aroma hops after 55 minutes.

15. Chill to 64°F (18°C).

continued

16. Transfer the wort into your fermentation vessel.

17. Pitch (add) the yeast.

18. Cover and leave for about 10 days to ferment.

19. After a week take a hydrometer reading. Hopefully, that should read in the region of 1.010 or lower. If it is higher, try moving it to a warmer spot or pitch some more yeast.

20. Bring ½ cup (125 ml) water to a boil and stir in the sugar. Allow to cool. Stir this into the beer with a sterilized spoon. Be gentle; you don't want to disturb the sediment.

21. Have a beer (optional, but advised).

22. Siphon into bottles or a keg. If using bottles, then don't forget to leave a little headroom and seal.

23. Leave the bottles for at least another week, if not two.

Bay, Rosemary, and Thyme Ale

YIELD: 5 gallons (20 L) ale   PREP TIME: 2 to 4 hours (over 2 to a few days)
MINIMUM FERMENTATION TIME: 4 days plus at least 1 week conditioning time

This beer is very simple to make because it uses malt extract. This means there is no need to go through the long process of mashing grains. It can also be made without much specialty equipment. Of course, if you have specialty brewing equipment, you should use it because it does make life easier. If you want to make this recipe using grains, simply use your favorite pale ale recipe and replace the hops with the bay and rosemary and use the thyme as the aroma.

The recipe is written so that it can be made both by those who are expert brewers and those who have no experience whatsoever. Please try not to be intimated by the terminology. As well, don't worry about the equipment—you can make a great beer without it. Beer, after all, has been made by humans without specialty equipment for thousands of years.

Strangely, the final product tastes of ginger. I suspect that the bay and/or rosemary have a terpene that can be found in ginger too.

INGREDIENTS

6½ gallons (24 L) filtered or unchlorinated water

7 pounds (3.1 kg) pale liquid malt extract

15 large rosemary sprigs

30 dried bay leaves

3 large thyme sprigs

12 ounces honey

One 0.35-ounce (10-g) package Mangrove Jack US West Coast Yeast M44 or at least 0.3 ounce (8 g) of any other ale yeast

1.4 ounces (40 g) sugar, for priming in a bucket, or ¼ teaspoon (1 g) in each bottle

continued

INSTRUCTIONS

1. If you have a wort chiller, bring the water to a boil and add the malt extract. Strip the rosemary and bay leaves into the water. Stir until the extract is fully dissolved and keep boiling for 30 minutes. If you are a novice brewer or if you don't have a wort chiller, you can boil half the liquid with the herbs and the malt extract. Then, at the end of the 30 minutes, pour in the rest of the water, ensuring it is as cold as possible.

2. During the last five minutes of the boil, add the thyme sprigs and stir in the honey.

3. Strain the liquid, which is now called wort, into a fermentation vessel large enough to hold 6½ gallons of liquid. If using a wort chiller, chill to below 68°F (20°C). The ideal temperature range to pitch the yeast is between 59 and 74°F (18 and 23°C). If you don't have a thermometer, it should be cool enough to leave your finger in without any discomfort.

4. Pitch your yeast by sprinkling it on top of the wort.

5. The gravity (if using a hydrometer) should be roughly 1.055. Leave for 4 to 14 days at 69 to 74°F (18 to 23°C) to ferment, or until around 1.012 on your hydrometer. The ABV will be 5 to 5½ percent, depending on how well your yeast has performed.

6. If using a bottling bucket, dump 1.4 ounces (40 g) sugar into it before siphoning in the wort over the top. If using bottles, then put roughly ¼ teaspoon sugar (1 g) into each bottle before siphoning in the

wort over the top. Leave roughly half an inch gap at the top of each bottle. Ensure that you leave the trub (sediment at the bottom) in the fermentation vessel. Leave the beer for at least a week to condition before drinking. The beer will keep for about a year.

CHAPTER 6

Fish, Meat, and Eggs

Throughout most of human history, successfully preserving high-protein foods like meat, fish, and eggs often made the difference between life and death. Luckily, our very survival no longer depends on preserving high-protein foods at home. Instead, these foods can now be an excellent and exciting extra on our dinner plates.

The leap from making a bit of sauerkraut to fermenting meat might seem rather large. Moreover, mistakes can result in a contaminated final product and perhaps a serious case of food poisoning. Therefore, I decided to keep to the basics and to offer recipes that don't need careful temperature and humidity control. The dishes that you can make using the recipes in this chapter are very tasty, and all of them can be made at home with the tiniest amount of equipment and expertise.

Pickled Eggs

YIELD: 6 eggs   SUGGESTED JAR SIZE: 1 pint (500 ml)
PREP TIME: 10 minutes (plus boiling time for the eggs)   FERMENTATION TIME: 3 to 5 days

Anyone who keeps or has kept chickens, or has lived near or is closely related to someone who keeps chickens, might wonder what to do with the abundance of eggs the hens produce. Fermenting eggs is an ideal way to keep that goodness until you actually need it, perhaps in the winter months when egg production slows down. Pickle those eggs throughout the year and never again will you say, "If I see one more egg! . . ."

Even if you don't keep chickens, I recommend giving this recipe a go, because pickled eggs are deliciously simple to make and the flavors can be adapted to your tastes.

In the UK, the best way to serve a fermented egg, also known as a pickled egg, is to open a bag of salted potato chips (crisps) and place the egg in the middle. In some places this is considered to be a worthwhile lunch that helps soak up the beer while playing darts.

INGREDIENTS

6 medium eggs (2 oz; 60 g each)

1 teaspoon sea salt

1 cup (250 ml) filtered or unchlorinated water (approximately)

Optional add-ins: garlic, dill, mustard seeds

INSTRUCTIONS

1. Place the eggs into a large saucepan, big enough not to have to pile them on top of each other.

2. Pour tap water over them, covering by 1 inch.

3. Heat the water until just boiling, then turn off the heat, put a lid on the pan, and leave the eggs in the hot water for 12 minutes.

4. Strain out the water and then leave to cool. Alternatively, you can plunge the eggs into cold water to cool them down a little more quickly.

5. While the eggs are cooling, make up the brine by adding the sea salt to the 1 cup filtered water.

6. Once cool, peel the hard-boiled eggs.

7. Place any flavorings you wish, such as garlic, dill, or mustard seeds, into the bottom of a clean jar. Pop the eggs in one by one. I find that six eggs just about fit when crammed into a 1-pint jar.

8. Pour over the brine and allow for ½ inch of head-space at the top of the jar. Cover with a small piece of material secured with a rubber band, and then place in your usual fermentation spot out of direct sunlight to ferment.

9. After three to five days, add the lid and transfer the eggs to the refrigerator and consume within two weeks.

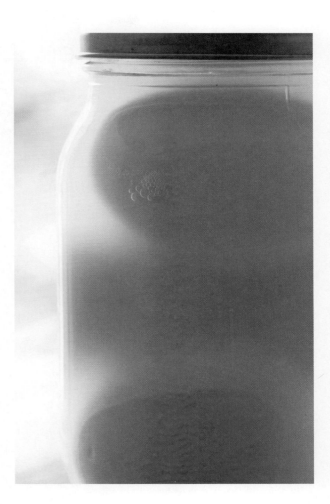

Pickled Kvass Eggs

YIELD: 6 eggs   SUGGESTED JAR SIZE: 1 pint (500 ml)
PREP TIME: 20 minutes (plus boiling time for the eggs)   FERMENTATION TIME: 3 to 5 days

This is a cute and colorful alternative to the recipe for Pickled Eggs (page 198). The result here is a more earthy tasting and pink pickled/fermented egg. You can of course add a whole bunch of other herbs and spices, just as you would with regular pickled eggs. A teaspoon of mustard seeds comes fully recommended!

INGREDIENTS

6 medium eggs (2 oz; 60 g each)

1 teaspoon sea salt

1 cup (250 ml) filtered or unchlorinated water (approximately)

1 cup Beet Kvass (page 152)

Optional add-ins: garlic, dill, mustard seeds

INSTRUCTIONS

1. Place the eggs into a large saucepan, big enough not to have to pile them on top of each other.

2. Pour tap water over them, covering by 1 inch.

3. Heat the water until just boiling, then turn off the heat, put a lid on the pan, and leave the eggs in the hot water for 12 minutes.

4. Strain out the water and then leave to cool. Alternatively, you can plunge the eggs into cold water to cool them down a little more quickly.

5. While the eggs are cooling, make up your brine by adding the sea salt to the 1 cup filtered water.

6. Once cool, peel the eggs.

7. Place any flavorings you wish, such as garlic, dill, or mustard seeds, into the bottom of a clean jar. Pop the eggs in one by one. I find that six eggs just about fit when crammed into a 1-pint jar.

6. Pour over your beet kvass and allow for ½ inch of headspace at the top of the jar. Cover with a small piece of material secured with a rubber band, and then place in your usual fermentation spot out of direct sunlight to ferment.

7. After three to five days transfer the eggs to the refrigerator and consume within two weeks.

Corned Beef

YIELD: 2 pounds (1 kg) corned beef   SUGGESTED JAR SIZE: 2 quart (2 L)
PREP TIME: 15 minutes   FERMENTATION TIME: 2 to 10 days

I once used to frequent a café just because I loved their salt beef bagels. Alas, the café went away when the owner decided to run a cake business instead. It now means that I have to make my own corned beef, and this is the recipe that I like to use. Corned beef is great in a Reuben sandwich or on a toasted bagel with lots of mustard.

The spice mix is my own favored recipe and is tailored around what I normally have on hand. Don't worry if you don't have all the ingredients listed here—you can make it with just salt. Some make it a little more warming and use cloves and cinnamon. Just let your own preference, and what you have in your larder, be your guide.

INGREDIENTS

One 2-pound (900 g) beef brisket or other boneless beef joint
2 tablespoons sea salt
1 tablespoon yellow mustard seeds
1 tablespoon brown sugar
1 tablespoon chili flakes
1 tablespoon dried juniper berries
1 tablespoon green peppercorns
1 tablespoon Sichuan pepper
½ cup liquid from a previous ferment
Filtered or unchlorinated water, enough to cover the brisket (roughly 1 quart)

INSTRUCTIONS

1. If the brisket has been in the freezer, let it thaw completely before using. I also like to bring it up to room temperature before starting work on it. Just make sure it is covered if doing this in the summer.

continued

2. Meanwhile, make the spice mix by adding all the spice ingredients together, then pounding with a mortar and pestle. Make 30 to 60 holes in the brisket with a skewer, turning once to make sure you get them in both sides.

3. Rub the spice mix thoroughly into the brisket and then pop your brisket into a 2-quart jar and pour enough water over to cover the meat. You need to leave a little bit of air space in the jar so that the bacteria have some oxygen, so move to a bigger jar if necessary.

4. You now have two options: First, you can leave the beef out to ferment at room temperature for two days or, second, you can pop it in the refrigerator for 5 to 10 days. I'd suggest using the refrigerator if you are in a hotter state or if it is the middle of the summer. Whichever method you choose, make sure you take it out of the jar and turn it twice a day so that it will evenly cure.

5. When the beef is ready, take it out of the jar and rinse it thoroughly. You can then slice it and put it in a sandwich raw. The first time I tried this it was really a leap of faith, but it is worthwhile. Pairing the raw corned beef with Rosehip and Horseradish Sauce (page 56) is nothing short of delicious. I also like to trim off the meat piece by piece and roll it into thin slices around big dollops of Cultured Mustard (page 85).

6. If not eating all straight away, refrigerate and use within one week

7. If eating fermented meat seems like a leap too far, the corned beef can also be cooked. Preheat the oven to 330°F (165°C). Rinse the brisket and then pat it dry. Put it on a wire rack fat side up and place the wire rack over a large roasting pan full of water.

8. Cover the pan with aluminum foil and pop it in the oven for two hours.

9. When you remove the pan, be very careful not to spill any water down you; if any is left it will be scalding hot. Wearing oven mitts, peel off the aluminum foil away from your face, as steam will rise from the corned beef.

10. Crank the oven up to 350°F (180°C) and return the brisket to the oven for another hour or until fully roasted. Enjoy with roasted vegetables, sauerkraut, and Fermented Horseradish Sauce (page 84).

Gravlax

YIELD: 3 pounds (1.5 kg) gravlax, enough for 12 people
PREPARATION TIME: 1 hour   FERMENTATION TIME: 1 to 2 days

The word *gravlax* means "grave fish"; *lax* meaning salmon and *grav* meaning, well, grave. This might sound like a rather odd name for a cured fish dish that tastes like an unsmoked version of smoked salmon. It makes more sense when you consider the origins of this dish, which is the Nordic countries of Northern Europe. People rubbed salt and sugar into fresh salmon, and then buried it while it cured. This would prolong the life of the fish from a good catch, if it wasn't all going to be eaten straightaway.

I found that a salt-to-sugar ratio of 2:1 by weight to be just right for this recipe. If you prefer a sweeter fish, you can alter this to 1:1 by weight. You can also add dill, fennel, or other herbs that complement salmon. I find that lemon balm and other delicate tasting herbs are overpowered by this fish, no matter how much I use, and so I think that using them for this preparation is a waste of herbs and effort. Another interesting twist on gravlax is to use spruce tips in the curing. These will give up their flavor if whole sprigs are pressed onto the fish along with the cure. Aim for spring/summer growth, as spruce then tends to be at its most flavorsome. You must be sure you are not picking sprigs from yew pine, however. Please refer to the foraging tips on page 50, and, remember, do not use anything you find foraging as an ingredient unless you are absolutely sure it is okay to ingest.

You can also add rum, vodka, or gin to the mix at a rate of roughly 1 fluid ounce per 3 pounds (30 ml) per 1.5 kg. There is fierce debate as to how traditional this technique is. Some swear by it, others say it doesn't make much difference to the final flavor. I'd suggest that it does. It can give the fish an extra flavor on what wine tasters call the *farewell*—the last

continued

flavor you are left with after eating. If you are hosting a dinner party with drinks that match, then I'd urge you to give it a go. It's not such a great idea if this is for a lunchtime treat and you have work in the afternoon!

As with all cured meat and fish, make sure the fish is as fresh as you can possibly find. Preferably, it will have been caught that morning. If filleting the fish yourself, be sure that any pin bones have been removed. For aesthetic reasons you can remove the skin too, although I like the skin and leave it on. Some like to work with a loin of salmon instead of a fillet, because the loin is of an even size and offers a more even final product. I personally like to have a little variation in flavor when I eat my gravlax. This ultimately comes down to personal preference.

If you are adapting the recipe, I would be wary of using an abundance of citrus juice. A little peel is fine, but if you start adding citrus juice to the fish before you cure it, then the acid in the juice will start to cook the fish. As a result you will end up with fish that is both cured and cooked, and it's not tasty.

INGREDIENTS

One 3-pound (1.5-kg) salmon fillet
½ cup (7 oz; 200 g) sea salt (see headnote above)
½ cup (3.5 oz; 100 g) sugar (see headnote above)
2 bunches dill (about 2 oz; 60 g; optional)
1 fluid ounce (30 ml) vodka/rum/gin (optional)

INSTRUCTIONS

1. If refrigerated, take the salmon out for about 30 minutes before curing. If you're going to, this is the point to take off the skin too.

2. Combine the remaining ingredients in a medium bowl to make the cure: for a simple cure that allows the fish to speak for itself, use just salt and sugar at a 1:1 volume ratio; in other words, ½ cup salt to ½ cup sugar. If using dill or other herbs, then finely cut them and add them to the bowl too. To help the flavor *open up* a little you can rub the ingredients together. This bruises the herbs, allowing for the flavor molecules to be released. If using rum/vodka/gin, then mix in with the cure.

3. Lay the salmon down on a piece of plastic wrap or cheesecloth and rub in the cure. Ensure that you cover the entire side of salmon as evenly as possible. It will start to soak into the fish straightaway, so I tend to rub a first layer in and then repeat until the cure stops immediately turning transparent.

4. Flip the fish over and repeat the process. Then wrap the plastic wrap/cheesecloth tightly around the fish, leaving the top and bottom free. Place the fish in a baking dish and place something heavy on top of it. I use jars filled with ferments, but if you don't have many, then try something else: a large, filled soda pop bottle or a heavy book or a chopping board with bricks on it for example.

5. Place the whole thing in the refrigerator and leave for at least 24 hours and up to 48 depending on how rich you like your fish. The fish will need turning at least four times when you do this. Drain off the excess liquid as you do so and keep the fish sealed in. If using cheesecloth, you may need to tighten it. The liquid that drains off can be kept in the refrigerator and made into a sauce for your fish.

6. Take out the now cured fish and rinse off the cure. This can be done by running it under the tap and rubbing it off with your hand. Some just brush it off but I find this far too salty.

7. To carve, take the sharpest and longest knife you have and cut in diagonal slices, the thinner the better. It takes practice, and the first two or three slices won't be very long as the angle gets deeper as you go.

8. Serve with cream cheese on a bagel or however you would serve regular smoked salmon. There is a discrepancy between many sources as to how long this dish will last in the refrigerator, and I have read anywhere from two to three days or up to two weeks. I have erred on the side of caution and will eat my gravlax within five days of curing it, and I have always been fine.

Note: This can be quite an expensive dish to make, depending on where you get your salmon. It can be scaled down, but the volume of cure will be altered, so just be sure the cure is evenly and liberally spread across the outside of the fish.

Fermented Fish Sauce

YIELD: 1 pint (500 ml) fish sauce   SUGGESTED JAR SIZE: 1 quart (1 L)
PREP TIME: 30 minutes   FERMENTATION TIME: 4 weeks

I've opted to use sardines for this recipe, but you might prefer mackerel, anchovies, or another oily fish instead. For a more intense flavor, simply ferment the fish for longer than I have recommended. For reference, the ancient Romans left theirs for several months until *the flesh fell apart*. I don't think you can use up old fish for this recipe—as with all ferments fresh is best. The smell is the first telltale sign of old fish. Is it overpowering? If so, it's too old. Also, check that the eyes are clear and not cloudy. You should press the flesh too—if it's fresh, it will spring back into place.

INGREDIENTS

1 pound (500 g) whole sardines (about 4 or 5 average sized sardines)

3 garlic cloves

½ teaspoon lemon zest or 1 sprig spruce tips

4 tablespoons sea salt

2 fresh bay leaves

1 teaspoon black peppercorns

2 tablespoons liquid from a previous ferment

1½ cups (375 ml) filtered or unchlorinated water, plus more if needed

INSTRUCTIONS

1. Chop up the fish into 1-inch (3-cm) chunks.

2. Transfer into a large bowl and firmly mash the fish. You'll feel the bones crushing beneath your masher.

3. To prepare the flavorings, peel and mince the garlic. Add the garlic and lemon zest or spruce sprig and the rest of the ingredients, except the water, in with the fish.

4. Transfer to a jar, cover with the water, and tightly close the lid. If there are fish poking out over the waterline, then add a little more water as required.

5. You can now leave it to ferment in a cool place away from direct sunlight, such as a larder, for four days.

6. After four days, move to the refrigerator and leave for at least two weeks and up to one month. The amount will be to your taste; the longer you leave it, the stronger the flavor—therefore if you want a really pungent fish sauce leave it for a month! The jar will need burping every four days or so. Check the top and if it is solid and popping up, then you need to burp it by opening the lid just a little. This is best done outside, as the smell can be quite overpowering!

7. Strain the jar into a pitcher through some cheese-cloth and sieve or colander. You may also want to do this outside.

8. The solids can now be used to make fish stock and the brown-red liquid is your fish sauce. It benefits from another, more fine, straining. Pour through a coffee filter into a 1-pint (500-ml) bottle. This can take some time.

9. Refrigerate the sauce; it should keep for about six months.

CHAPTER 7

Fruit

Sauerkraut, kimchi, beer, wine, and kefir are often the only foods that many folks ferment at home. Of course, it is no bad thing in and of itself. It must be said though that there is so much more to fermenting than this small handful of favorites. One aspect of fermenting that doesn't seem to get much attention right now is fruit fermentation. I hope the recipes on the following pages inspire you to explore this most rewarding and often overlooked landscape of tastes and textures.

If you are new to fermenting, I suggest you start with something simple, such as Fermented Apples (page 211). The process changes the taste of the apple while retaining its crisp bite; even the most bland and flavorless store-bought apple will become something you could imagine being served up in a Michelin-starred restaurant. If you are feeling a little braver, try Nabak-Kimchi (water kimchi; page 214). It is an exciting twist on the more traditional kimchi that you might know. I think the addition of the Asian pear is what makes this dish shine. You may wonder why these round fruits are so popular these days. It's because their crisp texture and slightly bland flavor allow them to dazzle when fermented. The Asian pear absorbs all the flavors found in the ferment, and so when biting into it you get a burst of everything. Nabak-Kimchi is something I like to snack on if I need to jolt myself out of that midafternoon slump.

There are a few key reasons why fruits don't always get a look in terms of fermenting. First, they don't keep for as long as fermented vegetables and other foods. Second, fruits can be a little harder to get right. These, however, are two obstacles that can be easily overcome.

The sugar content in fruit means a ferment is far more likely to produce alcohol, although sometimes this may be a bonus! If you don't want to get a little drunk when adding fermented cranberries to your morning cereal, then you should keep a close eye on your fruit as it is fermenting. I tend to give my fruit ferments a shorter period of time to ferment out of the fridge, especially in hot weather. I find that two days is plenty of time. If you are not sure, use your sense of taste as a guide. If the batch tastes sweet and not at all sour, then simply leave it out a little longer. If the batch starts to taste of alcohol, quickly put it in the fridge.

Another obstacle when making fruit ferments is what I call the *buoyancy factor*—since cranberries, blueberries, and other soft fruits float, you need to weigh them down. If you don't, then they will pick up some mold. You simply need to use enough weight so that the fruits don't poke over the waterline. Keep an eye on them, because sometimes the bubbles formed by the fermentation process will compound the *buoyancy factor* and push an inadequate weight clean off the top of your jar!

Fermented Apples

YIELD: 1 quart (1 L) apples   SUGGESTED JAR SIZE: 1 quart (1L)
PREP TIME: 10 minutes   FERMENTATION TIME: 3 days

Always use a crisp apple. Light-colored apples, such as Golden Delicious or Granny Smith, from late in the harvest are excellent. I suggest sticking to yellow and green apples because red ones do ferment, but they tend to be a little too mushy.

It is entirely up to you if you wish to peel your apples. My preference is to leave the skins on, because the most nutritious part is the skin. I also think that the flavor is vastly superior too—the skins add an extra dimension, a backbone to the sour tang.

It's up to you if you want to add spices. I much prefer eating a spiced version in the winter and fall. The plain version feels more like a spring and summer treat. Don't use powdered spices in this recipe, as the small particles are likely to attract mold.

INGREDIENTS

2 cups (500 ml) filtered or unchlorinated water

1 tablespoon sea salt

Optional add-ins: 1 cinnamon stick, 2 whole cloves, ½ whole nutmeg

Approximately 4 to 5 apples

INSTRUCTIONS

1. Make the brine by boiling ¼ cup (50 ml) of the water and stirring in the salt, then pour in the rest of the water and allow to cool. If using, add the spices to your quart jar.

2. Core, peel if you wish, and slice the apples into 1-inch-(3-cm)-thick wedges, and then pop them into the jar one by one. Try not to push them down too hard onto each other, as they will snap.

3. Pour over the brine and add a weight to stop the wedges from floating up.

4. Cover and leave to ferment—out of direct sunlight—for approximately three days. Once fermented, refrigerate, and eat within a month.

Fermenting the Fall Fruit Salad

YIELD: 1 quart fruit salad   SUGGESTED JAR SIZE: 1 quart (1 L)
PREP TIME: 5 to 10 minutes   FERMENTATION TIME: 2 to 3 days

Each of the fruits in this recipe are at their best in the fall around October. You may find it hard to get a hold of an Asian pear. If so, any kind of crisp pear will do. Do not use soft varieties of any of the fruit here, as they have a tendency to go mushy!

INGREDIENTS

1 cup (250 ml) filtered or unchlorinated water

1 tablespoon sea salt

2 persimmons

1 Granny Smith apple (or other crisp apple)

1 Asian pear (or other firm pear)

1 mint sprig

INSTRUCTIONS

1. Make the brine by boiling the water, then stirring in your salt and leave to cool.

2. Cut out the hard leaves from the top of the persimmons and then slice into quarters. Then core the apple and slice into 1-inch-(3-cm)-thick wedges. Cut the Asian pear in half and scoop out any seeds and surrounding pod. Cut into similar-sized wedges.

3. Place the fruit into your quart jar, alternating between the types of fruit you are putting in. Around halfway up put in the sprig of mint and continue to layer up the fruit.

4. Add a weight and cover loosely, then leave to ferment out of direct sunlight for two to three days. Refrigerate and enjoy within a couple of weeks.

Fermented Pomegranate Seeds

YIELD: 2 cups pomegranate seeds   SUGGESTED JAR SIZE: 1 quart (1 L)
PREP TIME: 5 to 10 minutes   FERMENTATION TIME: 3 days to 2 weeks, depending on preference

These are so simple and yet so addictive. I eat them straight out of the jar, or I stir them into homemade yogurt to give my breakfast a kickstart.

INGREDIENTS

2 cups pomegranate seeds (about 2 pomegranates, 7 oz; 400 g)
¼ cup (85 g) honey

INSTRUCTIONS

1. Deseed the pomegranates. I have two methods of doing this and both begin with chopping the pomegranates in half. With the first method, bang the fruit with a spoon until all the seeds drop out. For the second, submerge the pomegranates in water, then massage the seeds out. They float to the bottom and the pulp to the top. Pull out the pulp and peel, then filter through a sieve, picking out the last bits of pulp.

2. Pop the seeds into your jar, cover with honey, and seal.

3. Place them in a warm spot away from direct sunlight for at least three days and keep trying them until you are happy with the flavor—this also helps to *burp* the jar and stops the carbon dioxide from building up inside, sending shards of glass and fermented pomegranate seeds all over the place. Over time the seeds will get more and more alcoholic, reaching their peak at about two weeks. I personally think that they are nicer after five or six days, as the alcohol taste can become rather more like moonshine when left for longer. Also, after about day six the gasses really start to build up in the jar and you have to be constantly vigilant with the *burping* of it.

4. Once the seeds have fermented to your ideal level of alcohol, use just as you would regular pomegranate seeds. I like to serve them in salads or just eat as a snack. Refrigerate and eat within three months.

Nabak-Kimchi

YIELD: 2 quarts (2 L) nabak-kimchi   SUGGESTED JAR SIZE: two 1-quart (1-L) jars
PREP TIME: 1½ hours   FERMENTATION TIME: 6 hours to 2 days

According to New York–based Korean food master chef and YouTube sensation Maangchi, nabak-kimchi is best made in the fall. It's a fresh-tasting, fruity kimchi, and it was my first step into fermenting fruit.

The term *nabak* originated from *nabaknabak,* which means to flatten or thinly slice. This gives you an idea of how the radish should be sliced. The traditional version of this dish calls for minari (water celery), but I substitute with parsley stalks, because it proved impossible to find water celery. You could also use wild celery, which grows across all of the eastern states and much of the western and southern ones too. A word of warning if you are thinking about using this ingredient from the wild: Wild celery is easily confused with poison hemlock. Please refer to the foraging tips on page 6, and, remember, do not use anything you find foraging as an ingredient unless you are absolutely sure it is okay to ingest.

There are variations of this recipe, and all use fresh-tasting ingredients. This recipe is just my take. Think about adding cucumber or a fresh-tasting apple. I have even seen kombu (sugar kelp) used. When this ferment is eaten fresh there is quite a bit of heat, but that heat will die down as it matures. The fruit, however,

helps to counter the heat by balancing it with a sweetness. I think that when you eat nabak-kimchi you can feel it doing you some good!

INGREDIENTS

6 ounces (170 g) Korean radish

3 tablespoons plus 1 teaspoon sea salt

1 pound (500 g) Napa cabbage

4 cups (1 L) filtered or unchlorinated water

1 cucumber

2 green onions or spring onions

1 small green chili pepper

1 small red chili pepper

1 Korean (Asian) pear

1 crisp green apple

1 tablespoon thinly sliced onion

2 parsley stalks

2 garlic cloves, thinly sliced

1 teaspoon grated fresh ginger

2 teaspoons Korean hot pepper flakes

INSTRUCTIONS

1. Thinly slice the radish, place into a medium bowl, sprinkle over 1 teaspoon of the salt, and leave for an hour. Slice the cabbage lengthwise into quarters, then slice into pieces that measure 1 to 2 inches long. The idea is for them to be bite-sized, and that will depend on the size of your mouth! Put the cabbage into a separate medium bowl and pour over 1 cup of the filtered water. Leave for one hour.

2. Meanwhile, prepare the rest of your ingredients. Slice the cucumber into thin rounds, and cut the green onions into 1- to 2-inch sections, ensuring that you use all the onion and not just the white bit. Stem and slice the peppers. Peel the pear and core and slice both the apple and pear into 1-inch chunks.

3. Place the parsley stalks, onion, garlic cloves, grated ginger, and all the ingredients from step 2 into a big bowl and mix gently together.

4. Wash the cabbage in a colander or sieve. You need a delicate hand and not a heavy one in order to keep the crisp of the cabbage. Combine this with the fruit and vegetables.

5. Fill a medium bowl with 3 cups of the water and sprinkle in 3 tablespoons of salt. Tie the pepper flakes inside a small piece of muslin cloth and swim it around the 3 cups of water. You are looking to turn the water a reddish color without letting the flakes enter the liquid.

6. Combine the brine, fruit, and vegetables in an airtight container and leave until it has a tang in it—this could be as little as six hours or up to two days, according to your room temperature. I like to make it at night and eat it for an 11 a.m. snack.

7. Once fermented, keep refrigerated and eat within two weeks. After this time the fruit starts to discolor, and mold is more likely to start a party on the top of your fruit.

Preserved Lemons

YIELD: 1 pint (500 ml) lemons SUGGESTED JAR SIZE: 1 pint (500 ml)
PREP TIME: 10 minutes FERMENTATION TIME: 30 days or more

You may have seen some recipes for preserved lemons that replace the water with lemon juice. It doesn't make that much difference if you do this, but perhaps if you have a glut of lemons, you could give it a go.

Preserved lemons are popular in Morocco. The pulp is added to tagines and stews to give them an extra bit of zing. A lot of salt is used in the preparation, and if you use the pulp for cooking, you certainly won't need to add any more salt to the dish!

If you want to add more of that intense lemon flavor, it's the peel you are after. A few slices poked beneath the thighs or breast of a chicken or baked with fish is nothing short of heavenly. You can also use the juice/brine in dishes.

INGREDIENTS

4 to 6 unwaxed lemons

6 to 10 tablespoons sea salt

2 bay leaves (optional)

2 teaspoons black peppercorns (optional)

1 cinnamon stick (optional)

Filtered or unchlorinated water, as needed

INSTRUCTIONS

1. Slice the hard bits off the top and bottom of the lemons, down to the pith but not into the flesh. Quarter the lemons from the top to bottom but leave a ¼ inch at the bottom intact so that the lemons are still in one piece but can be made into a cross shape.

2. Cover the bottom of a pint jar with some of the salt—roughly 2 tablespoons.

3. Over a small bowl, liberally sprinkle about 1 tablespoon of salt per lemon in the heart of the lemons and then ram them into the jar one by one. After about three lemons, add the bay leaves,

peppercorns, and cinnamon stick, if using. Lemons vary greatly in size and while small ones will slip into your jar easily, rather big lemons may have to be halved in order to fit into the jar. I just use the blunt end of my rolling pin or a kraut crusher to push them in. Alternatively, you can make a bigger batch in a bigger jar or simply use a widemouthed jar.

4. Keep adding the lemons to the jar one by one until the jar is full. Push them tightly together; the less space between them the better. If the lemon juice hasn't risen to the top of the jar, top up with filtered or unchlorinated water.

5. Add yet more salt, 1 to 2 tablespoons, to cover the lemons.

6. Seal the jar and shake it. Place in a cool, dark place for 30 days, turning the jar daily. After that time you can start using them, just ensure you rinse them well before use. When you take out a lemon it is important to keep the rest covered with liquid. You can keep topping up with either filtered or unchlorinated water or lemon juice.

7. These will keep out of the refrigerator for up to a year (some say longer), though they may discolor to a brown. After a year they can be quite mushy and can be squished with the blade of a knife and used in sauces or condiments.

3-2-1 Citrus Marmalade

YIELD: 1 quart (1 L) marmalade   SUGGESTED JAR SIZE: 1 quart (1 L)
PREP TIME: 10 minutes   FERMENTATION TIME: 20 to 30 days

As far as I can work out, the origins of marmalade have always involved using something sweet, generally honey. This means the first marmalades were more like some kind of citrus mead. This recipe creates something that is a little more complex than the British breakfast staple loved by Paddington Bear—he might not even recognize it as marmalade!

The mix of fruit helps to balance the range of flavors they deliver. You can mix any citrus you get a hold of: kumquats, grapefruits, or limes are all possibilities. The flavors of the fruit are ramped up, so you may want to taste a little of each fruit together. This will give you a better idea of how they might come out before you combine them in the jar.

You can have a taste of the marmalade after a week or so, and some folks prefer it at this stage. I believe that it tastes much better when left for longer, as I think the strong flavors of the citrus fruit and the nuanced flavors from the peels mingle and amplify.

Keep refrigerated and use within a year. Serve your marmalade on strong, gamey meats or bake it into cakes.

INGREDIENTS

3 tangerines

2 oranges

1 lemon

2 cups (500 ml) filtered or unchlorinated water

½ tablespoon sea salt

INSTRUCTIONS

1. Dice all the fruit into chunks. Mix all of the bits of fruit together, then pop them into a quart (1 L) jar one by one.

2. Make up the brine by boiling your water, then stirring in the salt and allowing to cool. Pour it over your fruit.

3. Place a cover over the fruit and leave it in your usual fermentation spot out of direct sunlight to ferment.

4. Leave it for 20 to 30 days, or longer. You can refrigerate it, but I have left mine out for another two or three months and found it still quite pleasing.

Preserved Limes

YIELD: 1 pint (500 ml) limes   SUGGESTED JAR SIZE: 1 pint (500 ml)
PREP TIME: 20 minutes   FERMENTATION TIME: 30 days or more

My sister-in-law, Leia, is always in search for the perfect margarita, and she hates the trend toward using sugar instead of salt. I started making preserved limes just for her cocktails, with the intent of using the salted lime juice–flavored water from the ferment in place of the lime juice in those margaritas (see How to Make a Preserved Lime Juice Margarita, on the following page). I am hoping that she will be delighted with the results this Christmas. Preserved limes can also be used in sauces and marinades. Just like Preserved Lemons (page 216), the peel is the part that gets used the most when cooking.

INGREDIENTS

10 unwaxed limes
10 tablespoons sea salt
Filtered or unchlorinated water, as needed

INSTRUCTIONS

1. Slice the hard bits off the top and bottom of the limes, down to the pith but not into the flesh. Quarter the limes from the top to bottom but leave an ⅛ inch intact at the bottom so that the limes are still in one piece but can be made into a cross shape.

2. Cover the bottom of a pint jar with salt—roughly 2 tablespoons.

3. Over a small bowl liberally sprinkle about 2 teaspoons of salt per lime in the heart of the limes and then ram them into the jar one by one.

4. Push the limes tightly together; the less space between them the better. If you have a glut of limes and plenty of time, you can fill the jar with lime juice, if not, water will be fine.

5. Add yet more salt, 1 to 2 tablespoons to cover the limes.

6. Seal the jar and shake it. Place in a cool, dark place for 30 days, turning the jar daily. After that time you can start using them, just ensure you rinse them well before use. When you take out a lime it

is important to keep the remaining limes covered with liquid. You can keep topping up with filtered or unchlorinated water or lime juice.

7. These will keep out of the refrigerator for up to a year (some say longer); I've had some for eight months and in that time they discolored to a brown. After a year they can be quite mushy; the whole lime can be squished with the blade of a knife and used in sauces or condiments.

Note: Alternatively, you can make a margarita with the lime juice from this recipe, saving the peel of the lime to use in cooking.

How to Make a Preserved Lime Juice Margarita

YIELD: 1 margarita

PREP TIME: 5 minutes

There is no need to add salt to this margarita as there is plenty already inside the lime. I guarantee that this will make the most piquant margarita you have ever tasted—a word of warning though, they are devilishly moreish.

INGREDIENTS

½ ounce (15 ml) juice from Preserved Limes (page 220)
½ ounce (15 ml) Triple Sec
1 ounce (20 ml) tequila
1 ice cube
1 wedge of lime

INSTRUCTIONS

1. Carefully squeeze the lime juice from your preserved limes. I recommend plucking out one and shaking as much of the salty solution from it before you squeeze it. I'd also suggest gently squeezing it between your fingers. These limes are far softer than unfermented limes.

2. Add the triple sec, tequila, and preserved lime juice to your shaker along with the ice cube. Shake well; as a rule of thumb, I like to shake until my hand feels the cold of the ice cube coming through—about 30 seconds or so.

3. Strain into your margarita glass and garnish with a wedge of lime. Traditionally, you would rub the lime around the rim of the glass and rub the glass in salt; however, as it is already a salty drink there is no need—unless of course you are salt deprived!

Fermented Cranberries

YIELD: 3 cups cranberries   SUGGESTED JAR SIZE: 1 quart (1 L)

PREP TIME: 10 minutes or less   FERMENTATION TIME: 3 to 4 days

Just before Thanksgiving you might think you haven't got enough cranberries, so you start to panic, buying more. Just after Thanksgiving you start wondering what on earth you'll do with all the leftover cranberries! This recipe offers a simple solution to this issue, one that affects thousands of Americans every year. The result is a lovely tasting snack. These cranberries are really delicious, and they burst in your mouth with flavors that form a bridge between Thanksgiving and Christmas.

INGREDIENTS

12 ounces (340 g) cranberries

1 cup (250 ml) filtered or unchlorinated water

1 tablespoon sea salt

2 tangerines

3 tablespoons raw honey

1 tablespoon liquid from a previous ferment (optional)

1 teaspoon pumpkin pie spice

Large pinch of sumac powder (optional)

Zest from ½ lemon

INSTRUCTIONS

1. Pop the berries into a quart jar.

2. Make a brine by boiling the water, adding the salt, and allowing to cool. Meanwhile, juice the tangerines and add the juice along with all the other ingredients to your jar, then add the cooled brine.

3. I would usually suggest using weights for fermenting, as I don't really like using plastic. However, as many of us know, cranberries float due to the tiny pocket of air inside them (it's how they harvest them), and they often push the weights out of place. It is far better to leave a 1-inch (3-cm) gap at the top of the jar, large enough to fit in a water-filled zip-top bag. This keeps the pesky little fellows submerged and forms a seal.

4. Place your jar in your usual fermentation spot to ferment for three to four days.

5. Once the cranberries have fermented, they can be stored in the fridge and are best eaten within three months—but I'm sure they won't be around that long!

Fermented Blueberries

YIELD: 1 cup (200 g) blueberries   SUGGESTED JAR SIZE: 12 ounce (340 ml) if available, 1 pint (500 ml) if not
PREP TIME: 5 to 10 minutes   FERMENTATION TIME: 4 days

This recipe is inspired by the one from the world-renowned Danish restaurant Noma. My adaptation adds a little zest from a lemon. I think this adds to the overall result. Feel free to leave this out, or swap the lemon peel with lime, tangerine, or orange. Blueberries pair really well with a bit of citrus.

INGREDIENTS

2 cups (200 g) blueberries

Scant 1 teaspoon (4 g) sea salt

2 inches (5 cm) lemon peel (optional)

INSTRUCTIONS

1. Pour the blueberries into a bowl and sprinkle the salt over them. Move the bowl back and forth so that the blueberries all get a good coating of salt.

2. Transfer the salted blueberries and the lemon peel, if using, into a 12-ounce (340-g) jar and weigh them down with a weight or water-filled zip-top bag.

3. Cover the jar loosely with a piece of material.

4. Leave the jar in a warm spot for four days, longer if it's cold—let their taste be your guide. The juice will have started to extract out, and it should rise to higher than the level of the blueberries. Remember, you are waiting until the berries have that characteristically sour taste.

5. Separate out the juice from the fruit. The berries will keep for a few days in the refrigerator or for much longer if you wish to freeze them. The resulting berries can be eaten just as you would normal blueberries—in smoothies, on cereal, or just as a snack. Strangely, I think they take on some of the characteristics of blackberries—perhaps it's the deepening of flavor.

Note: *My favorite way of serving these blueberries is with bacon on a morning pancake. The leftover liquid is also very pleasant neat, similar to Beet Kvass (page 152), and it is great when mixed to make a cocktail. I've used it at a ratio of 2:1:1 with sour mash whiskey and apple cider vinegar.*

Fermented Morello Cherries

YIELD: 3 cups (340g) cherries   SUGGESTED JAR SIZE: 1 quart (1 L)
PREP TIME: 30 minutes to 1 hour   FERMENTATION TIME: 3 to 4 days

Sitting proudly in front of our house is a dwarf morello cherry tree. Throughout early summer we are blessed with a great crop of cherries year after year with very little effort. This means we can have winter cocktails garnished with a little piece of summer.

I tried preserving sour cherries with just brine, but the taste was not for me. The addition of honey or sugar helps to lift the sour taste to something far more pleasant. You can also add other spices such as bay, chili peppers, and peppercorns. This does, however, limit what the cherries will pair with once done.

The most obvious way to consume the final product is in a cocktail, such as a Kir Royale. But they can also work very well on a cheese board. I especially like them with ripe, soft French cheeses. You could also try them with your morning yogurt for a double-fermented kick to start your day.

INGREDIENTS

12 ounces (340 g) morello or sour cherries
1 cup (250 ml) filtered or unchlorinated water
1 tablespoon sea salt
3 tablespoons raw honey or equivalent sugar
1 tablespoon liquid from a previous ferment (optional)

INSTRUCTIONS

1. Pit the cherries. This is so much easier with a cherry pitter, but you can place the cherry over the neck of a bottle and push down with a chopstick as an alternative.

2. Make a brine by boiling the water, stirring in the salt and sugar, and allow to cool. Place the cherries in your quart jar and pour the liquid from a previous ferment over them.

3. I would usually suggest using weights for fermenting, as I don't really like using plastic; however, cherries can float. It is far better to leave a 1-inch (3-cm) gap at the top of the jar, large enough to fit a water-filled zip-top bag. This keeps the pesky little fellows submerged and forms a seal.

4. Place the jar in your usual fermentation spot to ferment for three to four days, stirring occasionally. Refrigerate and use within six months.

Fermented Spruce Tip Rhubarb

YIELD: 1 quart rhubarb   SUGGESTED JAR SIZE: 1 quart (1 L)
PREP TIME: 2 minutes   FERMENTATION TIME: 3 to 5 days

Rhubarb is best grown at home, rather than bought in the grocery store. Its crowns can be planted in the spring, and it is important to leave them for a year or preferably two before you harvest from them. Doing so will help the rhubarb get used to its new home. Your patience will be rewarded each and every spring with a supply of rhubarb from this low-maintenance crop. If new to using rhubarb, always remember that the leaves are poisonous—don't use them!

If you aren't able to grow your own, then check out farmers' markets and specialty stores for your supply of rhubarb. Alternatively, you can ask on social media. Quite often growers find they have a glut of rhubarb and are delighted to give them up.

The addition of spruce tips, or indeed pine needles, in this recipe gives the rhubarb an earthy, citrus flavor. Please be sure that you

are not picking poisonous yew pine. For foraging tips, see page 50. If you are not close to a coniferous tree or are unsure about what you are picking, you can substitute the spruce tips with extra zest from a lemon. The best time to pick spruce tips and pine needles is in the spring, which luckily is right in the middle of rhubarb season. Aim to pick the brightest green or greenish-yellow shoots of spruce, as these pack the most flavor.

If you are feeling brave, then you can experiment with a few different types of tree (each tree has its own distinct flavor). Again, you must be sure of what you are picking. Avoid picking near any major roads or from contaminated land.

This recipe will help you enjoy rhubarb throughout the year. I like to mix mine with Stilton cheese and place them on oat cake crackers.

INGREDIENTS

2 cups (500 ml) filtered or unchlorinated water
1 tablespoon sea salt
10 ounces (300 g) rhubarb stalks
1 spruce sprig or a scant handful of pine needles
2 bay leaves
1 tablespoon liquid from a previous ferment (optional)

INSTRUCTIONS

1. Make up the brine by boiling ½ cup of the water and then adding the salt. Top up with the rest of the water and ensure it is at room temperature before using.

2. Cut the rhubarb so that each piece measures about 6 inches (15 cm). Plop these into a quart jar along with the few odd ends you will have no doubt cut off.

3. Wedge the spruce sprig or pine needles and bay leaves behind the rhubarb in the jar so that they are pressed against the side.

4. Pour over the brine until it covers the rhubarb. You may need to use a weight if the rhubarb hasn't wedged in the jar.

5. Add the liquid from a previous ferment if available—don't worry if you don't have any, as your ferment will soon get started without.

6. Cover the jar loosely with a piece of material or an airlock and place it out of direct sunlight to ferment for three to five days.

7. Once it has fermented, keep the jar in the fridge. You can eat the stalks straightaway, but I recommend leaving them for a little bit longer as this enhances the flavor. Use within six months.

Lacto-Lemonade

YIELD: Just under 2 quarts (2 L) lemonade   SUGGESTED JAR SIZE: 2 quart (2 L)
PREP TIME: 20 minutes   FERMENTATION TIME: 3 to 5 days, sometimes longer

Naturally fermented lemonade is often made the same way as Ginger Beer (page 154) and Turmeric and Cardamon "Beer" (page 157). For this recipe I tried something a little different instead: lacto-fermenting.

This recipe is a simple riff on an American classic, and it can be made without too much effort. Don't expect the same lemonade you already know so well, as this is lacto-lemonade and its taste is altogether different. It can be scaled up very easily—this recipe is for a small batch that makes just two bottles.

The keen-eyed reader might notice that I have put *sometimes longer* as a fermentation time. This is not because I haven't measured it, it's because I have found that lacto-fermented drinks can be a little sluggish to get started. My first batch of lacto-lemonade took a month to really get going. I have concluded that this was due to cold weather, as they all started bubbling away when the mercury started to rise. However, under the right conditions, this recipe usually ferments for three to five days.

INGREDIENTS

6 cups (1½ L) filtered or unchlorinated water

1 cup granulated sugar or honey

1 cup of freshly squeezed lemon juice

2 tablespoons liquid from a previous ferment

INSTRUCTIONS

1. Boil 2 cups of the water and stir in the sugar. Pour into a quart container and then allow to cool before adding the lemon juice and starter culture.

2. Cover loosely with a tea towel or small piece of material and leave in a warm place for three to five

days. You want to see some activity before moving on to the next step. If you don't see any bubbles, move your container to a warmer spot. Be patient; it can take a while to get started.

3. Once it has fermented, pour into the bottles and keep refrigerated. Ensure that you burp the bottles every few days or just drink it really quickly.

4. If the fermentation stops, add a teaspoon of sugar for every 2 cups' worth of lemonade.

Lacto-Fermented Orange Juice

YIELD: 3 cups (1½ pints; 750 ml) orange juice   SUGGESTED JAR SIZE: 2 quart (2 L)
PREP TIME: 20 minutes   MINIMUM FERMENTATION TIME: 3 to 10 days

Fruit juices have been on the firing line from health officials due to their high sugar content and lack of insoluble fiber. It has even been said that calorie for calorie, fruit juice is worse for you than fizzy soft drinks. But fear not, fermenting the sugars means that you can still enjoy your favorite juice and all of its health benefits without overloading your system with sugar.

Store-bought pasteurized orange juice can be used in this recipe, and it is a great way of bringing an otherwise dead product to life. That said, I find the best results come from freshly squeezed orange juice.

Every recipe I have found for lacto-fermented orange juice is a slight variation from the classic Sally Fallon's recipe from her landmark cookbook, *Nourishing Traditions*. My version is a fairly basic recipe, perhaps one of the easiest in this book. You can vary it with any juice. I've also tried it with whey and the juice from a red cabbage sauerkraut (see Sauerkraut, page 136). The sauerkraut worked better, and it also turned the liquid a lovely crimson red.

INGREDIENTS

3 cups (750 ml) fresh orange juice
2 tablespoons starter culture, such as whey
1 teaspoon sea salt

INSTRUCTIONS

1. Put all the ingredients into your 1½-pint (750-ml) jar and seal. Leave for 3 to 10 days to ferment. The variation depends on how warm your house is and just how tart you like your juice. The longer you leave it, the more sugar will be fermented and the tarter your drink.

2. You will need to burp it now and then to ensure that pressure doesn't build up inside the jar.

3. Once the juice has fermented to your satisfaction, bottle and keep refrigerated—refrigeration slows down the fermentation and reduces the likelihood of explosion.

Note: The resulting drink has more depth of flavor than a regular orange juice. As someone who occasionally suffers from acid indigestion, I find that normal orange juice upsets me in the mornings. However, I can drink the lacto-fermented orange juice until the cows come home.

Fermented Plum and Fig Brandy

YIELD: 3 cups brandy plus 1 pound 8 ounces (750 g) fruit   SUGGESTED JAR SIZE: 1 quart (1 L)
PREP TIME: 10 minutes   FERMENTATION TIME: 5 days to 2 weeks

This recipe could possibly be one of the oldest in the book; it is simple and very delicious too. For an even tastier version, try using wild figs and plums instead of store bought.

INGREDIENTS

8 ounces (250 g) figs

1 pound (500 g) plums

1½ (500 g) cups raw honey or 1½ cups granulated or
   1½ cups brown sugar

1½ cups brandy

INSTRUCTIONS

1. If picked wild and you are certain there is no pesticide or pollution contamination, there is no need to wash the fruit. If in doubt or you are using store-bought fruit, then wash it.

2. Sterilize your quart (1 L) jar. Cut the figs in half, pit the plums, and destem both the figs and plums. I find the best way to pit the plums is to cut them into quarters; the stone should pull out. Overripe plums may take a little more persuading!

3. If using honey, then stack up the fruit inside your jar and slowly pour the honey over them. It is a fairly slow process but immensely satisfying. If using sugar, mix in a bowl beforehand, ensuring that the sugar covers all of the plums. Stack up the fruit inside your jar.

4. Leave a 1-inch gap at the top of your jar and then press the fruit down with a weight or water-filled zip-top bag to keep the fruit from floating up. I also tie some cheesecloth or a piece of fabric around the top of the jar.

5. Place your jar somewhere that keeps at around room temperature and leave for five days to two weeks. The length of time depends on preference as it will get more alcoholic and have more of a kick with time. Over the next few days the sugar or honey will start to draw liquid out of the plums and this will rise up in the jar. This can then seep out and drip down the side of the jar; I advise putting a plate under it. I also advise to keep an eye on the cheesecloth and replace it if necessary.

6. After fermentation is complete separate the fruit from the liquid by straining through a fine mesh sieve or cheesecloth—do not squeeze the fruit, as this can cause haze. You can eat the fruit with a little ice cream or even the brandy. My preference is to cover it in melted chocolate, let it cool, then serve with a glass of the liquor.

7. The liquid can now be drunk neat or mixed with the brandy. I find that once mixed it makes an excellent plum Brandy Alexander! Once you have added the brandy, if free of any debris, it should keep for up to six months in the fridge. After that time it will still be drinkable, but it can start to lose its full flavor.

Tepache

YIELD: 4 quarts (4 L) tepache   SUGGESTED FERMENTATION VESSEL: crock
PREP TIME: 10 to 15 minutes   INITIAL FERMENTATION TIME: 2 to 3 days
SECONDARY FERMENTATION TIME: 2 days

This recipe makes use of the leftover bits of a pineapple, and for a fermented drink, it is pretty quick and easy to make. I'd suggest this recipe for anyone who wishes to find an easy route into fermenting drinks.

Some tepache recipes call for the whole pineapple (barring the top leaves). Others suggest just the skin and core of the pineapple but not the flesh. I find that using just the skin and core to be the best approach, because using the flesh tends to give the drink a vinegar flavor.

This recipe uses a whole pineapple and will produce a gallon of tepache. You can half or even quarter the recipe if this is too much.

INGREDIENTS

1 pineapple

1 gallon (4 L) filtered or unchlorinated water (approximately)

1 pound (500 g) brown sugar or 1 large piloncillo cone or 1 pound (500 g) honey

INSTRUCTIONS

1. Slice the top and bottom off the pineapple. Discard the top. Roughly cut off the skin, cut in half, and then take out the rough central core.

2. Place the pineapple (including the skin and core) into a 1-gallon crock. Meanwhile, boil 1 quart (1 L) of the water and mix in the sugar. Top up with the rest of the (cold) water and pour over the pineapple.

3. Leave to ferment at room temperature for two to three days. Small bubbles should have appeared

on the surface of the water. If there is a little bit of scum on the surface of the water, scoop it off.

4. Strain out the pineapple chunks and core. Then bottle into six 26-ounce (750-ml) flip-top bottles. If you like your tepache to have some fizz, seal and leave for another two days for secondary fermentation. Keep refrigerated and drink within a week.

Cider

YIELD: Variable

PREP TIME: 2 hours   FERMENTATION TIME: 8 weeks

Cider, also known as hard cider, has been made for thousands of years by many different peoples. According to Dan Crissman, author of *Brewing Everything*, Johnny Appleseed was not planting apple trees to make apple pie. Instead it was for the frontiersmen who needed a steady supply of fruit for their cider mills. Cider came over to the United States from England, and apples were considered to be one of the first crops grown in the New World.

Over in the UK, from the Middle Ages until fairly recently, many farm laborers were paid in cider (or cyder as it was known). This practice occurred across many of the patchwork counties that make up England. Apparently, some laborers became quite the connoisseurs and would only work for the best cider makers.

The farm owners had their work cut out for them, because making hard cider is easy but making good cider isn't. I can explain how to make cider in one phrase, in fact in just five words: squeeze apples, ferment the juice. The only trouble with making cider like this is that you don't really have much control of the final taste. With just a little more care and attention you can start creating cider that would have had farm workers queuing around the block, or rather haystack, to dig your fields.

You'll notice that, unlike the rest of the recipes in this book, I don't mention the amount of apples needed or the yield. This is because both depend on how good your juice extraction method is and how juicy the apples are. That said, as a rule of thumb 20 pounds (9 kg) of apples should make around 1 gallon (4.5 L) of cider.

INGREDIENTS

Apples (see headnote)

INSTRUCTIONS

1. Choose the apples. Depending on where you live there might be very little choice, and you will have to go for store-bought. I've made very good cider using a mixture of eating apples and cookers. However, if you can get a hold of decent cider apples, then you really should use those. These can be hard to come by, especially in the United States.

2. Wash the apples. They don't need a really good scrub, just get rid of any dirt that you see on the skins.

3. Cut the apples. Unless you are making cider in a large quantity you can get away with cutting the apples into quarters or eighths, depending on their size. When dealing with larger quantities of apples, you will benefit from making or buying a scratter. This is a specialty piece of equipment that cuts up the apples mechanically; it can be bought at some specialty stores or online.

continued

4. Press or juice the apples. I have made cider using apple juice obtained from juicing the apples. This is a great option that shouldn't be overlooked. If you wish to invest further, apple presses are available that will get the juice out far more quickly. Check your local homebrewing store or the Internet.

5. Strain the apples. Once juiced or pressed the juice can be poured through a piece of cheesecloth into your sterilized fermentation vessel.

6. Fermenting. Leave the juice to ferment for about eight weeks. You'll know when it is ready because it will have stopped bubbling. Take a reading with a hydrometer if you have one; it should read 1.000 or thereabouts. As long as it gives a consistent reading over two to three days you are okay to move on to the next step.

7. Bottle or keg. Siphon the cider off the sediment on the bottom of the fermentation vessel. You can siphon into a jug or bottling bucket before pouring into bottles, as this will make your life a little easier. Leave roughly a ½ inch of space at the top of each bottle. Alternatively, you can siphon into a keg, which is a much better option for bigger batches.

8. You can drink the cider right away; however, it will benefit from at least a month left in a cool place to condition.

Plum Wine

YIELD: 5 gallons (19 L) wine   SUGGESTED FERMENTATION VESSEL: crock
PREP TIME: 1 to 2 hours, longer if you include picking the plums
MINIMUM FERMENTATION TIME: 10 days and an additional 4 months

Plum wine is made across much of Asia, but it differs from this wine as the Asian wine is often really just an infusion of plums in alcohol. This version is one of my favorite country wines. It is made by extracting juice from the plums, rather like Fermented Plum and Fig Brandy (page 234).

You can use any plums that you get your hands on. My preference is to get as many different sorts and freeze them across the growing season. As long as your plums add up to the weight of 20 pounds (9 kg), you are good to go. Freezing them also breaks the skin, meaning they will be easier to ferment.

The addition of bananas might seem a little odd, but I have found that they add body to a wine. They work well with lots of other stone fruit wines too. If you find the grape concentrate hard to get a hold of, you can substitute it by boiling down a quart of store-bought grape juice.

When it comes to adding the yeast I suggest using a high-tolerance wine yeast, as plums can contain a lot of sugar. Opting for a yeast like a Red Star Pasteur Blanc, for example, will make a drier wine. If sweeter is your preference, then perhaps go for Red Star Côte des Blancs, as this will ferment at a slightly lower percentage. Do be aware, however, that even using Côte des Blancs will ferment to around 14 percent ABV—this can be a strong wine!

If your preference is to make an all-natural wine, you can substitute the sugar for honey. You could even try making this wine without using store-bought yeast—instead leave your must (unfermented wine) out and wait for the yeast on the plums to get to work.

continued

This natural yeast approach will create a sweeter wine, because it is unlikely you'll harvest a yeast that will fully ferment all the sugars. It does make for quite a nice tasting drink. Just place the fruit into your fermentation vessel along with the water and stir every day. It will start to bubble. After a few days the bubbling will stop. Simply decant it into carboys and leave it to condition, or go ahead and drink it straightaway.

INGREDIENTS

20 pounds (9 kg) assorted plums
5 gallons (19 L) filtered or unchlorinated water
13 pounds (6 kg) sugar or 16 pounds (7.5 kg) honey
2 overripe bananas
1 cup (250 ml) grape concentrate
5 teaspoons pectic enzyme
5 teaspoons yeast nutrient
One 0.176-ounce (5 g) packet high-tolerance wine yeast
  (see headnote above)

INSTRUCTIONS

1. Sterilize your fermentation vessel.

2. Unless using overripe plums, freeze and thaw the plums.

3. Boil the water and stir in the sugar until fully dissolved. Turn off the heat and add the plums, bananas, and the grape concentrate. Allow to cool to around 68°F (20°C), then stir in the pectic enzyme and yeast nutrient.

4. Finally, sprinkle the wine yeast over the must and leave loosely covered in temperatures ideally 75 to 80°F (21 to 24°C).

5. Leave for 10 days. About every two days return to it and mash the fruit with a sterilized wooden spoon or plastic masher.

6. After 10 days, strain into a 5-gallon carboy and attach an airlock. Fill the airlock with vodka or another high-strength spirit. Leave for about another month. I find this wine can create a lot of sediment, and depending on how high the sugar content is in the plums, it can continue to ferment for a long time. I therefore recommend racking the carboys at least once. That means siphoning out

the must (unfermented wine) from the lees (the sediment) into another carboy. If you don't have another carboy, you can siphon back into your washed and sterilized fermentation vessel and then back into your carboy—remember to reattach the airlock each time.

7. When the airlock has finally stopped bubbling, your wine is ready to be bottled. Again, siphon off the lees when bottling.

8. The best way to cork the wine is by using a corking machine, available from most good homebrew suppliers. I have found screw-top and flip-top bottles don't keep the wine for very long, and it soon turns to vinegar—especially in a house with so many other things fermenting.

9. Condition for around three months before drinking. The wine should keep for about five years.

CHAPTER 8

Dairy

I first visited Romania back in the early 1990s, and I was struck by the timelessness of the area. Great plains were peppered with haystacks held together with fallen tree branches. Villagers would barter their homegrown vegetables for cheese and eggs with local small holders, and people still walked their cows up and down the high streets. Village life, at least in the places I visited, seemed like it had remained unchanged for thousands of years.

In fact, new evidence is suggesting that some of the scenes I saw in Romania were first seen over 7,500 years ago. And that those farming the cattle there were some of the first people to develop the lactase enzyme that now allows 35 percent of the world to drink milk without fear of it coming back out their noses.

Back in 2009, a team at University College London used a computer simulation model to explore the spread of the lactase enzyme in humans. Lactase is the enzyme responsible for the breakdown of lactose, the sugar in whole milk. This enzyme is produced in the lining of the small intestine. It is estimated that 65 percent of the world's population doesn't have it, meaning they react rather badly to milk products.

Yet, it was over 11,000 years ago—some 4,000 years before these milk-swigging Romanians—that the first cows were domesticated and used for dairy farming. Thousands of years is a long time for human beings to suffer from abdominal pain, bloating, flatulence, and nausea due to consuming milk products. I suspect that they didn't—I suspect that they had thousands of little helpers in the form of bacteria cells that digested those sugars for them. A look at the many indigenous communities that farm dairy herds across our great planet adds weight to this theory. From the yak milk in Tibet, to skyr in Iceland, jocoque in Mexico, and blaand in Scotland, all these foods have two things in common: they are all made of milk and they are all fermented.

Crème Fraîche

YIELD: 1 cup (250 ml) crème fraîche   SUGGESTED JAR SIZE: 1 pint (500 ml)
PREP TIME: 10 seconds   FERMENTATION TIME: 2 to 3 days

Isigny-sur-Mer, in Normandy, France, with its population of less than 4,000 and mishmash of architectural styles, might seem like a rather unremarkable small French town. Yet, like so many European towns, it punches well above its weight in the culinary ring. The town is fed by four rivers and is surrounded by lush green grasslands, making it ideal territory for rearing cattle. Home of Camembert cheese, this town also produces my favorite butter and creates the best crème fraîche in the world. This crème fraîche is thicker and richer than many of its competitors, partly due to the local bacteria culture, and it features its own distinctly sharp, slight acid flavor. Although crème fraîche this good can be difficult to buy, as it is sold only in larger gourmet grocery stores and on the Internet, it is ridiculously easy to make.

INGREDIENTS

2 tablespoons buttermilk or live yogurt

1 cup (250 ml) heavy cream

INSTRUCTIONS

1. Place the buttermilk into a glass jar and pour the cream over it. Mix well, then cover with a paper towel or dish towel and secure with a rubber band. This step works to keep any flying critters, rogue dust particles, and pesky microbes at bay.

2. Set your jar where it won't get knocked over for two to three days or until it starts to thicken and has the desired tang.

3. Once it is ready, replace the lid and refrigerate. It should last for almost two months. It's a wise move to keep back 2 tablespoons of crème fraîche for your next batch.

Fresh Curd Cheese

YIELD: Up to 6 ounces (170 g) cheese

PREP TIME: 30 minutes   FERMENTATION TIME: 2 to 3 days

For this recipe I enlisted the help of Tom from Burt's Cheese (burtscheese.co.uk), a small artisanal cheese maker based in Cheshire, England. Tom teaches a course in cheese making, and this is one of the most basic of cheeses that people make during the course.

The rennet and mesophilic starter can both be bought online. For details on where to find cheese-making equipment and starter cultures, please refer to the resources on page 276.

INGREDIENTS

1 quart (1 L) unhomogenized whole milk

One 0.08-ounce (2½-g) packet mesophilic starter

½ teaspoon rennet

Few drops filtered or unchlorinated water

½ teaspoon sea salt

Herbs (optional)

INSTRUCTIONS

1. The first step is to make sure all the equipment used is clean; this can be done with a mild sterilant solution such as Star San.

2. Fill your medium saucepan with water and place a nonbreakable bowl so that it fits neatly over it.

3. Pour the milk into the bowl and heat to 86°F (30°C). Take off the heat and stir in the mesophilic starter.

4. Cover and leave for two hours.

5. Place your pan (and bowl) back on the heat and bring back to 86°F (30°C).

6. Dilute the rennet with a few drops of filtered or unchlorinated water and stir it into the milk. Keep stirring for at least one minute to ensure that they are fully combined.

7. Leave for 18 hours at room temperature. The curd is ready when it has sunk below the whey.

8. Using a large spoon, carefully ladle the curds into either molds or a colander lined with muslin and allow to drain for 12 to 24 hours at room temperature.

9. The curds should now have a tangy/lemony flavor. To make a spreadable cheese, mix the curds in a bowl with the salt (add more depending on taste). If you so desire, other ingredients, such as herbs, can be mixed in at this point.

10. The cheese is now ready, and it will keep for about a week in the refrigerator. You can make the leap and make a cheese that holds its shape at this point. Leave the cheese in the mold or colander and sprinkle a small amount of salt on the top. Then carefully turn it out onto your hand and salt the rest.

11. Return the cheese to the mold for a few hours, and it will take on the shape of the mold. Traditionally, the cheese would have been wrapped in leaves at this point. You can even soak the leaves in kombucha, beer, cider, or anything that you wish to impart a flavor to your cheese.

Fromage Blanc

YIELD: 1 quart (1 L) fromage blanc

PREP TIME: 20 minutes   FERMENTATION TIME: 1 hour

The term *fromage blanc* means white cheese in French. This cheese is similar to Quark (page 252) in many ways, but due to the cream it has a bit more fat in it. Serve it as you would crème fraîche, as it is excellent with strawberries!

INGREDIENTS

2 quarts (2 L) whole milk

1 cup (250 ml) half-and-half or single cream

2 cups (500 ml) buttermilk

2 tablespoons freshly squeezed lemon juice, plus more if needed

¼ teaspoon sea salt, plus more if desired

INSTRUCTIONS

1. Pour the milk and half-and-half into a large saucepan.

2. Slowly raise the temperature of the milk, stirring occasionally. Keep track of the temperature and when it reaches 175°F (80°C) take it off the heat.

3. Combine the buttermilk, lemon juice, and ¼ teaspoon salt in a separate bowl, then pour that into the saucepan. Gently stir and then leave it for 12 minutes. This should curdle straightaway, giving you curds and whey. If it doesn't curdle, or you notice only one small clump of curdled milk, then keep adding a little more lemon juice until it does.

4. Line a colander with cheesecloth and pour the contents of the saucepan through it. I find that most of the liquid goes through when you first pour. If you wish to retain this whey, place it over a bowl. Remember, it will make a great protein-packed drink and can also be frozen for later use or used to make pancakes.

5. For the next 30 to 40 minutes the whey will slowly drain away. To finish off this process, wrap your cheesecloth around the cheese, making a ball of cheese. Twist the end of the cloth, then suspend the ball above a large bowl until it stops dripping. The aim is to keep the ball off the bottom of whatever it is draining into.

6. Once drained, scrape out the cheese and add salt to taste. You can now place your cheese into a ramekin or similar small bowl. Cover and leave it out for a few hours to ripen. Your cheese can now be refrigerated and eaten within a week.

Quark

YIELD: 1 pint (500 ml) quark SUGGESTED JAR SIZE: 1 quart (1 L)
PREP TIME: 10 minutes FERMENTATION TIME: 2 to 3 days

The origins of quark are lost to antiquity, but the smart money suggests that it came from somewhere in middle or northern Europe (the word *quark* originates from the German language). This cheese is kind of a cross between yogurt and cream cheese and can be used as either.

Store-bought quark can often be bland and tasteless. If that is all you have tried, please do give it another go with this recipe, as the real stuff has a much more pronounced flavor.

INGREDIENTS

1½ pints (750 ml) whole milk
1 cup (250 ml) cultured buttermilk

INSTRUCTIONS

1. Pour the milk into a medium saucepan and heat until bubbly; you may need to stir it a few times to avoid scalding the milk. When it has started to simmer, take it off the heat and allow to cool to room temperature.

2. When cool enough, pour into a quart jar and add the buttermilk. Put on the lid and shake until well mixed.

3. Leave in your usual fermentation spot out of direct sunlight for 24 hours. After this time it should have become the consistency of yogurt. Have a taste to ensure the culture got to work; it should have the unmistakable tang of microbes.

4. Next, you need to strain. I find that most of the liquid goes through when you first pour, so the best plan of action is to line a strainer with cheese-cloth, set it over a deep bowl, and pour the mixture through. Once most of it has strained you will be left with a little ball of cheese. To strain out the last of the liquid, wrap the cheesecloth around the ball of cheese and twist the end of the cloth. Place the twisted end over the lip of a large jar and either twist around a wooden spoon so that it balances over the top or wedge a lid over the cheesecloth. You are aiming to keep the ball of cheese off the bottom of the jar to leave space for the whey to drain off freely. It strains through very slowly and might take overnight, so you'll need to place in the refrigerator or larder while it drips out.

5. When you open your refrigerator in the morning you should now have quark and some whey. It will keep in a smaller jar or other airtight container for roughly a week. The leftover whey can be used to make yogurt or another dairy fermentation. Personally, I like to keep a little to drink with my breakfast; it is rich in protein and it helps fill you up for the day.

6. Use the quark within a week. I love quark on an oat cake with a little piece of tomato on top of it.

Kefir

YIELD: 1 pint (500 ml) kefir   SUGGESTED JAR SIZE: 1 pint (500 ml)
PREP TIME: 10 seconds   FERMENTATION TIME: 24 to 48 hours

I share an office with a bunch of writers and musicians. It's a cultured environment in more ways than one! When I told the always immaculately turned-out musician Nicky of my not-so-secret fermentation passion, she admitted to a kefir habit. The next day she brought me a strange, brainlike substance in a jar. These little clusters of yeast and bacteria were to become my first step into dairy fermentation, and what an easy first step it was.

Luckily, kefir grains are becoming relatively easy to come by. Check the resources section on page 276 (or just ask local musicians!).

INGREDIENTS
1 tablespoon kefir grains
1 pint (500 ml) whole milk

INSTRUCTIONS

1. Place the kefir grains in the bottom of a clean 1-pint jar and top up with milk. Shake and then leave to ferment for 24 to 28 hours, shaking now and then. The grains will multiply, and the milk may even separate, hence the shaking.

2. After 24 to 48 hours, it's time to strain the kefir into a bottle or second jar. If you don't want to eat lumpy bits of kefir grains, then you should strain out the multiplied grains. I use a funnel with a built-in strainer for this job and all you have to do is swirl your finger around the funnel as you pour.

3. You can keep the grains aside for your next batch, although I have developed a taste for them and eat them raw—they taste rather like a funny kind of goat's cheese! You can keep reusing the grains indefinitely, but freshly made kefir should be used within three weeks.

Fermented Butter

YIELD: 3 ounces (90 g) butter   SUGGESTED JAR SIZE: 1 pint (500 ml)
PREP TIME: 30 to 40 minutes   FERMENTATION TIME: N/A

I was so impressed with my first batch of fermented butter that I wanted the world to taste it. In practice this meant giving some to all my friends. My friends are more prone to being honest than polite, and they all raved, as I did, about it. I still want to "spread" this butter across the world and urge you to make some.

INGREDIENTS

1 cup (250 ml) chilled Crème Fraîche (page 247)

Ice (optional)

Sea salt

INSTRUCTIONS

1. Dollop the crème fraîche into your food mixer bowl and mix for about 30 seconds, or in a butter churn and mix for around 30 minutes, until it separates. It helps to keep the crème fraîche as chilled as possible throughout the process; you can do this by living in Anchorage, Alaska, and going outside, or by using ice to keep the bowl chilled. At the end of this process you will now have cultured butter and buttermilk, the liquid being buttermilk.

2. Pour the buttermilk through cheesecloth and a funnel into a clean bottle, then refrigerate. You can use it for baking a variety of dishes, including soda bread or your morning pancakes.

3. Strain the rest of the butter through the cheesecloth. I tend to really press down on the butter, as the more buttermilk you can get out, the longer the butter will keep; but if you are refrigerating it, use it within three weeks.

4. Mix in the salt to taste. If refrigerating, keep it covered. You can also freeze butter if you wish to make it in bigger batches. Although, I'd suggest not telling your friends, as you'll have none left.

Long Viili

YIELD: 1 pint (500 ml) long viili   SUGGESTED JAR SIZE: 1 pint (500 ml)
PREP TIME: 10 seconds   FERMENTATION TIME: 24 hours

The inhabitants of the Nordic countries of northern Europe have a passion for more than just facial hair, heavy rock music, and woolen clothes. They also love fermented milk products, and most people there consume about 3½ ounces (80 g) of the stuff every day. One of the most popular is viili, a mesophilic yogurt that originates from Finland.

The world *mesophilic* comes from mesophile, meaning an organism that grows in moderate temperatures, between 68 and 113°F (20 and 45°C), to be more exact. This means that your viili will culture at room temperature, making this an easy "countertop" yogurt.

Although it can be difficult to get a hold of a starter culture for viili anywhere outside of northern Europe, you can order some from the Internet and from specialty food stores. Once you have made a batch you can, with just a spoonful of the previous batch, make the next batch. This means if you develop a taste, you'll never have to be short again (that is, unless your household is like mine and contains two children who will eat the last of anything that even resembles yogurt).

One of the most remarkable things about viili is how it binds together. If you spill a bit, the whole lot might slowly follow it like some strange being from *Star Trek*.

INGREDIENTS

1 teaspoon viili starter culture (see headnote)

1 pint (500 ml) fresh whole pasteurized milk (not UHT)

INSTRUCTIONS

1. Stick the starter culture into a 1-pint jar and pour over the milk. Stir well, then cover with a small piece of material and secure with a rubber band.

2. Leave in a warm place, avoiding drafts and temperature fluctuations, for 12 to 18 hours. You'll know when it is done, as the contents of the jar will have become a single mass that will pull away from the jar as you tilt it.

3. Place in the refrigerator for six hours before eating. This will keep the cultures intact for making more.

4. Unlike some ferments, viili tastes pretty mild, so it can be transformed by having flavors added. You could try fruit, jellies, honey, maple syrup, or my personal favorite: a spoonful of cocoa powder. Do remember to spoon out some before you do this for your next batch.

5. Keep refrigerated and use within one week.

Yogurt

YIELD: 2 quarts (2 L) yogurt   SUGGESTED JAR SIZE: two 1-quart (1-L) jars
PREP TIME: 15 minutes   FERMENTATION TIME: 8 to 12 hours

You don't have to buy a yogurt maker to make yogurt. The whole yogurt-making process can be accomplished using items found in most kitchens. This process is, after all, at least 1,000 years old.

INGREDIENTS

2 quarts (2 L) whole milk, raw or pasteurized
2 tablespoons fresh live yogurt culture
Ice (optional)

INSTRUCTIONS

1. Pour the milk into a large saucepan and heat until it reaches 180 to 200°F (82 to 93°C); at this point it will have started to bubble. Just as you would when making hot chocolate, heat gently; you don't want the milk to boil over or to burn on the bottom of the pan. This process changes the protein structure of the milk so that it will set as a solid.

2. Next, let the milk cool to 100°F (43°C). In order to do this, fill up a sink with iced water, place the saucepan in it, and keep stirring until it reaches the magic temperature of 100°F (43°C). As our sink is near a window, I also keep that open when it's cold outside. You could also just leave it for around an hour, checking the temperature frequently.

3. If you don't have a thermometer, then you can put your finger in the milk. If you can keep it there for the count of "two Mississippi" without it hurting, it should have reached the desired temperature. Make sure you don't make the mistake of letting it cool too much, as the cultures won't work quite so well.

4. Meanwhile, pour 2 quarts (2 L) of boiling water into an insulated cooler, swish it around, and then drain. This helps to warm up the cooler, which will hold the temperature, be it hot or cold. This helps to create the ideal environment for your yogurt culture.

5. Mix in the starter yogurt culture with the milk and pour into two 1-quart canning jars. Cap and place in the cooler. Fill any gaps between the jars with towels or any spare garments you might have and place the cooler in a warm spot. Some people don't use a cooler; they simply cover their canning jars with a quilt to keep them warm. Just do what you can to keep them from getting cold. Rest assured, if your yogurt has a green layer of water on top, it is fine! If it is runny, it's fine too. Don't worry: it will set in the refrigerator.

6. Check after 8 to 12 hours; it should be thick, tangy, and delicious by that point. Keep refrigerated; it will keep for three to four weeks.

Greek Yogurt

YIELD: 1½ quarts (1.5 L) yogurt
PREP TIME: 2 to 3 hours   FERMENTATION TIME: N/A

Greek yogurt is nothing more than yogurt with the whey taken out. It is simple to make, and I guarantee that the Greek yogurt from this recipe will taste better than any you have bought at the supermarket.

INGREDIENTS

2 quarts (2 L) yogurt (page 260)

Dairy **262** Fermenting Everything

INSTRUCTIONS

1. Pour the yogurt into the cheesecloth and fold in the four corners. Turn the cheesecloth so you have a ball and secure with the string. Place the ball in a bowl, as the liquid will be escaping. Let it drain for two to three hours.

2. Spoon out the contents into containers.

3. Keep refrigerated and use within a week. Keep back a tablespoon for your next batch of yogurt.

CHAPTER 9

Desserts

It is true that there are not many fermented desserts out there, but they do exist. At any rate, it didn't seem fitting to finish the recipe section of this book without including at least a couple. These are by no means the only fermented desserts out there, but they are both very tasty and pretty easy to make. On top of that, they are suitable for vegetarians and can be adapted for vegans without compromising on taste. I hope that, if you have worked through every recipe in turn, you will find these two as a little treat at the end.

Sweet Potato Poi

YIELD: 1½ pounds (700 g) sweet potato poi
PREP TIME: 2 minutes   FERMENTATION TIME: 24 to 72 hours

This traditional Hawaiian recipe is usually made from the underground part or corm of the taro plant. I couldn't come by any corm, and I understand that it can be hard to come by in the United States, so I used sweet potatoes instead. You may find that the sweet potatoes in your local store are mislabeled as yams. If you are unsure, just ask the store clerks. Another confusing point is that both yams and sweet potatoes can have orange and white flesh. Again, if you are unsure you should ask.

In some versions of this recipe other ingredients are added, such as coconut milk, cinnamon, maple syrup, and brown sugar. I find the dish to be fine without these additions, but don't be afraid to experiment.

INGREDIENTS

3 sweet potatoes (about 1 lb 8 oz; 700 g)

1 tablespoon liquid from a previous ferment (if available)

½ teaspoon sea salt

½ cup (125 ml) filtered or unchlorinated water or milk or coconut milk, if needed

INSTRUCTIONS

1. Cook the sweet potatoes until really soft; this can be done several ways. My preferred method is to cut them in half (so they fit), then pierce them several times, and put them in my pressure cooker for 25 minutes. Piercing them is essential, as they can explode in your face when you take the lid off your pressure cooker. They can also be steamed for about 25 minutes or oven baked for 40 minutes at 350°F (180°C). In both cases don't forget to pierce them. If oven baking, do not forget that sweet potatoes have a tendency to leak, covering the

bottom of your oven in hot, sticky goo that forms a solid lump, which is impossible to get off. To avoid this, put a baking sheet or pan on the shelf below to catch the lavalike drips. Whichever cooking method you choose, use a fork to check that they are done; there should be very little resistance when pushing it into the flesh. In fact, they should almost fall apart. If they are a little firm still, then cook for a little longer.

2. Once cooked, place them in a large bowl. I like to pick them up with tongs, as they can be mighty hot—be careful. Using the back of a wooden spoon, mash the potato, skin and all, until the sweet potatoes are mashed.

3. Allow to cool to room temperature, then stir in the liquid from a previous ferment, if using, and the salt. Cover and leave to ferment for 24 to 72 hours.

4. Once fermented, place in the food processor or blend with your hand blender until it becomes a smooth paste.

5. You can add some or all of the water (or milk or coconut milk, for a little flavor) and serve as a side or dessert.

Fermented Cashew Nut "Cheese" Cake

YIELD: 1 "cheese" cake

PREP TIME: 2 to 5 minutes (plus 8 to 12 hours soaking time)   FERMENTATION TIME: 5 days

I have to admit I struggled with the title for this recipe. I mean, it is not cheese because it is made with nuts, but I couldn't really call it Fermented Cashew Nut-product Cake, either. It doesn't have quite the same ring to it.

We can lose the enzyme that helps us break down lactose in the body as we grow older. This is one reason why you don't see many adults drinking a pint of milk at a bar. I, therefore, wanted to develop a recipe for my lactose-intolerant and dairy-free readers, but I couldn't quite bring myself to put it in the dairy section.

The resulting nut cheese can be mixed with herbs and flavors of your choosing. This "cheese" cake is surprisingly tasty, but it still isn't cheesecake.

INGREDIENTS

For the cashew cheese

2 cups (200 g) cashew nuts

Filtered or unchlorinated water (for soaking nuts)

2 tablespoons liquid from a previous ferment

Sweet baklava flavor

1 tablespoon raspberry jam or 1 tablespoon honey or 1 tablespoon maple syrup

1 drop vanilla essence

Enhance the nuttyness

Large pinch ground cinnamon

Zest of ¼ orange

For the "cheese" cake

4 broken graham crackers or ¾ cup chopped pistachio nuts

1 ounce (30 g) butter or 3 dried figs

2 cups cashew cheese (see above)

Strawberries, halved, for garnish

INSTRUCTIONS

1. For the cashew cheese: Place the nuts in a medium bowl and pour over the water; cover and leave to soak overnight.

2. Drain out the water and pour the liquid from a previous ferment over the nuts. If using a hand blender, blend the nuts in the bowl, or transfer them to a food processor. Blend until it becomes smooth, like the consistency of hummus.

3. Transfer the blended nuts to cheesecloth and hang it over a bowl, leaving them to drain for 48 hours.

4. Transfer your drained cashew cheese to a bowl and mix in any herbs or flavors that you are using.

5. If you are making cheesecake, skip this step and move on to step 6. If using as cheese, shape into whatever shape you find the most pleasing—rolling it to a log shape is possibly the easiest, but there is no reason why you can't roll it into a ball. Cover with parchment paper and then transfer to an airtight container and place in the refrigerator. Although you can eat it straightaway, it will benefit from a little more aging—around five days should be enough. Once aged, eat within five days.

6. There are a number of options when you flavor your cheesecake. You can make it either sweet and let it become more like baklava, the famous Ottoman dish; or you can take a different route and enchance the nuttiness to make something that is less sweet and altogether delicious. For the baklava flavor: Transfer the "cheese" into a bowl and add your chosen flavors for the sweetness—add the jam, honey, or maple syrup and the vanilla essence. For enhanced nuttiness: Transfer the "cheese" into a bowl and stir in the cinnamon powder and orange zest. For both flavors, keep stirring until fully combined.

7. To make the "cheese" cake base, throw the graham crackers or pistachios into a food processor and mix until you have crumbs or powder. Melt the butter in a small pan, being careful not to let it burn, or chop up the dried figs. Add them to the processor and keep blending; I find that if using pistachios, the mix keeps sticking to the blades, so you may have to unclog it a few times to get the desired consistency. You will be left with a semi-solid base. Transfer to a small plastic tupperware—the kind your sandwiches might be stored in. Push it into the base, ensuring it is about ¼ inch (2 cm) thick.

8. Place the cashew cheese on top of the base and then place the tub in the freezer for at least two hours. Allow to thaw for 15 minutes before serving. To serve, score the cheese cake into the desired amount of pieces, then scoop them out while still frozen. It is quite rich, so although it might seem like a small amount for all of this effort, you don't need much to satisfy.

9. This will keep in the freezer for at least three months, but who wants to wait that long for cheese cake? It also pairs well with soft fruit, so strawberries can be added for garnish.

CHAPTER 10

Problem Solving, Further Reading, and Resources

I hope that after making some of the recipes in this book you will want to learn more about fermenting. I have researched this topic extensively, and this chapter lists some of the books and websites that I found to be invaluable. Some of the ingredients and equipment you need to ferment foods can be a bit difficult to find in more mainstream stores, so I have also listed a few suppliers that should be able to help you. This chapter begins with some of the common problems that you might face when fermenting, along with some advice to help you on your way.

Fermented Foods: Are They Safe to Eat?

If you keep your ferments at the right temperature, add enough salt, use clean equipment, keep the contents of your jars submerged in liquid, and use good-quality ingredients, then you shouldn't have a problem. Break any of these rules and you might run into trouble with mold.

Trust your nose when it comes to testing your fermented foods. If your fermentation smells so bad you can't bring yourself to eat it, then guess what? It is bad and you shouldn't eat it.

Mold can present itself in a variety of colors. It can also look fuzzy, slimy, or fluffy. If the consistency of the fermentation has changed for the worse, then it is time to discard.

Blue mold can arrive in small colonies. You might see it on a pot of jam, for example. If you catch these early enough, you can skim off the top layer. See how far down it has penetrated, rid yourself of any contamination, and then leave your ferment out for a little longer while keeping a close eye on it. If you find any more signs of contamination, then you will have to throw away your ferment and start again.

My very first attempt at sauerkraut resulted in a furry mold. This was because the cabbage was in contact with air. I skimmed off the mold and then made sure the cabbages stayed below the surface of the liquid, and it turned out fine.

Here is the general rule: If, after you have skimmed off the mold and the ferment is fine in a couple of days and doesn't stink or taste bad, then you should be okay. If the mold comes back or the ferment starts to smell really bad, then you need to get rid of it.

Yeast Infections

It's not uncommon to find a white film on your fermentation. This isn't a mold, but a yeast known as kahm yeast. I find this yeast is most likely to occur during the summer months. Years of practice have taught me to ferment as much as I can by the end of the spring. I avoid fermenting most things when the temperature of my kitchen heats up, and so I wait until fall when possible. If I want to ferment produce that only grows in the summer—I move the ferment to the coolest spot I can find in my house.

Kahm yeast is also likely to occur when your ferment doesn't get acidic enough, when you haven't used enough salt, or if your ferment is exposed to too much oxygen. In mild cases you can skim off the yeast and discard any food that it has touched. The rest will be safe to eat. If your whole batch smells bad, and there is a heavy infection, then you should discard the ferment and start again.

Once you have rescued a ferment from an infection of kahm yeast, the next step is to minimize the chances of it coming back. To do this, wash any weights you are using, empty the jar, and place the contents into a new jar. Add a bit more salt or brine, and perhaps consider using an airlock. Last, make sure you put your ferment in a cooler spot.

Black Liquid

Sourdough starters need regular feeding. If a layer of harmless black liquid forms on your sourdough starter, it means that you have left it too long and it has gotten hungry and is turning into alcohol. Simply tip off the liquid and discard about 75 percent of the starter and start looking after your sourdough!

Problem Solving: Alcoholic Drinks

Every summer my inbox bulges with emails from people who have made a mistake while making elderflower champagne, a traditional English drink that is typically made from the flowers of the black elder tree *Sambucus nigra*. (For a recipe, see Alcoholic Elderflower "Champagne" on page 70.) Luckily, most of the time these problems are easy to solve, as they tend to fit into a few categories, all due to bacterial infections caused by lack of cleanliness and yeast problems.

These problems can occur when making most any alcoholic drink. An exception, of course, is when you are hoping for a bacteria infection, as in the case of Boza (page 184)! With that caveat, here is how to

solve the typical problems that may arise when you make alcoholic drinks.

FERMENTATION DOESN'T START

It can be really frustrating when you have gone to all the effort to make a drink, especially a beer, only to find that it doesn't ferment. The most obvious cul-prit is the yeast. It's a good practice to make a yeast starter or, if using dry yeast, to activate it before starting. Most good yeasts will have instructions on how to do this on the back of the packet. Otherwise, just mix tepid water with a little sugar and sprinkle it over the yeast. It should start to bubble after about 10 minutes. If it doesn't, or if the bubbling is lacklus-ter, then you have dead yeast.

Too much sugar or too little acid can also inhibit yeast growth—double-check the recipe and adjust accordingly.

It's also possible you could be fermenting somewhere that is too cool. This slows down and even stops yeast growth. Check the temperature and move the ferment to somewhere warmer than 64°F (18°C).

STUCK FERMENTATION

Stuck fermentation is when your drink tastes overly sweet. Take a hydrometer reading if you can to test the sugar level.

Check the temperature. It needs to be above 64°F (18°C) for fermentation to happen. I find that a good shake seems to work sometimes—simply pick up your carboy or fermentation vessel and shake vigorously.

As with fermentations that do not start, your fermentation may also have too much sugar or not enough acid. Check the acid level with pH strips and then adjust by adding citric acid or the juice of a lemon. Check the sugar level with a hydrometer and dilute if you need to.

EXPLODING BOTTLES

Some drinks are more prone than others to explo-sions. Lacto-fermented juices, for example, rely on being "caught" mid-ferment in order for them to have some fizz. This makes them volatile because they release carbon dioxide, which builds up inside the bottle. Don't be afraid; with a little pre-caution they can be tamed.

First, before you bottle, if a drink looks like it is fermenting pretty vigorously, with foam coming out of the airlock or so many bubbles that it makes a bot-tle of champagne look flat, then leave it to ferment for a few days longer until this stage of vigorous fer-mentation has subsided. You are asking for trouble otherwise, as your bottles will soon fill with carbon dioxide and they will explode.

Next, always use strong flip-top bottles, as they are designed to flip open when the pressure builds. The last step is to keep the bottles cool. The refriger-ator is the best place for them, as the cool tempera-tures will slow down fermentation. I have found that, quite often, lazy fermentations can start up again when winter turns to spring. The extra few degrees make all the difference. If storing drinks between these seasons and out of the refrigerator, then please do keep a close eye on them.

Further Reading

FOOD AND DRINK FERMENTATION

Booze for Free, Andy Hamilton, Plume, 2013

Brewing Everything: How to Make Your Own Beer, Cider, Mead, Sake, Kombucha, and Other Fermented Beverages, Dan Crissman, The Countryman Press, 2018

Kaukasis: A Culinary Journey through Georgia, Azerbaijan & Beyond, Olia Hercules, Weldon Owen, 2017

Nourishing Traditions: The Cookbook that Challenges Politically Correct Nutrition and Diet Dictocrats, Sally Fallon, NewTrends Publishing, 1999

Pickled, Potted and Canned: How the Art and Science of Food Preserving Changed the World, Sue Shephard, Simon & Schuster, 2006

Preserving Everything: Can, Culture, Pickle, Freeze, Ferment, Dehydrate, Salt, Smoke, and Store Fruits, Vegetables, Meat, Milk, and More, Leda Meredith, The Countryman Press, 2014

Real Food Fermentation: Preserving Whole Fresh Food with Live Cultures in Your Home Kitchen, Alex Lewin, Quarry Books, 2012

Sacred and Herbal Healing Beers: The Secrets of Ancient Fermentation, Stephen Harrod Buhner, Brewers Publications, 1998

The Essential Book of Fermentation: Great Taste and Good Health with Probiotic Foods, Jeff Cox, Avery, 2013

The Naked Guide to Cider, James Russell and Richard Jones, Tangent Books, 2015

The Noma Guide to Fermentation: Including Koji, Kombuchas, Shoyus, Misos, Vinegars, Garums, Lacto-Ferments, and Black Fruits and Vegetables, René Redzepi and David Zilber, Artisan, 2018

The Perfect Pint: A Beer Lover's Handbook, Andy Hamilton, Bantam Press, 2018

Wild Fermentation: The Flavor, Nutrition, and Craft of Live-Culture Foods, Sandor Ellix Katz, Chelsea Green Publishing, 2003

FORAGING

Edible Wild Plants: A North American Field Guide to Over 200 Natural Foods, Thomas Elias and Peter Dykeman, Sterling, 2009

Identifying and Harvesting Edible and Medicinal Plants in Wild Places, "Wildman" Steve Brill and Evelyn Dean, HarperCollins, 1994

Incredible Wild Edibles, Samuel Thayer, Foragers Harvest Press, 2017

The Encyclopedia of Edible Plants of North America: Nature's Green Feast, Francois Couplan, Keats Publishing, 1998

The Forager's Feast: How to Identify, Gather, and Prepare Wild Edibles, Leda Meredith, The Countryman Press, 2016

The Forager's Harvest: A Guide to Identifying, Harvesting, and Preparing Edible Wild Plants, Samuel Thayer, Foragers Harvest Press, 2006

Wild Drinks and Cocktails: Handcrafted Squashes, Shrubs, Switchels, Tonics, and Infusions to Mix at Home, Emily Han, Fair Winds Press, 2015

Wild Edibles: A Practical Guide to Foraging, with Easy Identification of 60 Edible Plants and 67 Recipes, Sergei Boutenko, North Atlantic Books, 2013

Web Resources

Archive.punkdomestics.com: This used to be a community-run site that was buzzing with life. It is now sadly a static archive resource, yet it is still full of great recipes and fun articles.

Cleverguts.com/forums: Fairly active forum, often with opinions on the latest fermentation news stories.

Ferment.works: Authors Kirsten and Christopher Shockey suggest you upload photos of your fermentations to understand what is going on. A good, simple idea that has become a valuable resource.

Maangchi.com: One of my favorites. This site is by a New York–based Korean housewife who became a YouTube sensation. Her site is a great resource for all things Korean food.

Phickle.com: A cute blog written with warmth. It includes many recipes from author Amanda Feifer.

Theotherandyhamilton.com: Foraging, fermentation, brewing, and me.

Wildfermentation.com: One of the oldest resources out there. It features a web forum and blog posts. Recently, there is more activity on the Facebook group Wild Fermentation.

WHERE TO SOURCE INGREDIENTS

Bellabeanorganics.com: Organic vegetables direct from the suppliers.

Farmboxdirect.com: Vegetable box scheme that links farmers directly to customers.

Farmfreshtoyou.com: Another very good vegetable box scheme.

Japansuper.com: Japanese food delivered worldwide.

Kalyx.com: Online resource for buying salt and other dry ingredients in bulk.

Maangchi.com/shopping: Maangchi's comprehensive list of Korean stores worldwide.

Misfitsmarket.com: What happens to all the misshapen vegetables? They end up at Misfits Market, where you can grab yourself a whole heap of fruits and vegetables for cheaper than you can at many stores.

Saskmade.ca: Great Canadian resource for boxed vegetables, wheat, and even Canadian-grown lentils!

EQUIPMENT, STARTER CULTURES

Cheesemaking.com: Starter cultures for cheese and a whole lot more.

Closetcasepatterns.com/the-ultimate-list-of-online-fabric-stores: As the link says, a list of fabric stores worldwide. A great place to get muslin, which works out to be cheaper than cheesecloth.

Culturesforhealth.com: Starter kits and jars, crocks, and some recipes to boot.

Fermentaholics.com: Run by "fermentation fanatics" who promise the best cultures at affordable prices. Includes bottling resources too.

Joann.com: A great place to search for cheesecloth.

Midwestsupplies.com: Carboys and more across the Midwest.

Nwferments.com: Kefir, yogurt, and much more. You can also find starter cultures and some great videos too.

Standingstonefarms.com: Kombucha and cheese starter cultures, plus a variety of workshops on offer throughout the year.

YEAST AND HOMEBREW EQUIPMENT

Northernbrewer.com: A long-running favorite of mine. Everything you need to get you started, a great selection of yeasts, and plenty of articles archived to inspire the would-be brewer.

FORAGING RESOURCES

Foragers-association.org.uk/members: Although UK–centric, some of the best foraging teachers in the United States, and indeed the world, are members of the Association of Foragers. Each and every member is vetted before they are allowed to join.

Foragersharvest.com: Sam Thayer is a great wild food educator. He and his friends run courses in Wisconsin throughout the year.

Wildfood.in: Attempting to be a worldwide wild food map.

Wildfoodschool.com: Online resource for plant education in the United States.

ACKNOWLEDGMENTS

Thanks, first of all, to Emma, my partner, who allowed me to take over the kitchen (once again) and who put up with the smells and clutter associated with the increase in fermented food and drinks around the house. To my children, Loki and Lark too, who didn't poke around too much in my experiments!

This book would not have gotten off the ground if it wasn't for my agent Kate Johnson, who went above and beyond what is expected of an agent, even recruiting her parents to help!—thanks Kate (and Kate's mom and dad).

I must also give a huge thank you to Roy Hunt, my friend and photographer, a true gentleman whose kind nature and good manners made him a pleasure to work with.

Thanks to my friends in my writing room, Lon Barfield, Becci Golding, Mike Manson, Richard Jones, Joe Melia, Jo Darque, Nicky Coates, and Mark Steeds for listening to me enthuse about bacteria and fermentation with good humor and grace. Extra thanks need to go to Nicky Coates for the endless supply of kefir grains, and to Richard Jones for his expert advice on cider. And, of course, to my forager friends who helped out here and there: Lisa Cutliffe of Edilus Wild Foods, Martian Bailey (a.k.a. Mavin Dainsbury of GoForaging), Richard Mawby, and, of course, Edible Craig Worral.

Thanks to Olia Hercules and my Latvian neighbor, Daiga, for introducing me to fermented tomatoes. Also, thanks to Tom Partridge for his help with the cheese recipe, and to Wizzy and Sky Kong Kong for helping me understand just what kimchi means to Koreans.

More thanks to Róisín and Ann, my editors, for their part in this whole process, and to Isabel for her good humor and grace. I write this before I know everyone else at The Countryman Press who will be involved, but I feel truly blessed to have been able to write this book and so I thank you all.

* *Italics* are used to indicate illustrations.